THE
TOUR DE FRANCE
MISCELLANY

*This book is dedicated to my wife Janice and my two sons,
Marc & Paul.*

*Without their love and support, this book would never have
been possible.*

This edition published in 2013

Copyright © Carlton Books Limited 2013

Carlton Books Limited
20 Mortimer Street
London W1T 3JW

A CIP catalogue record for this book is available from the British
Library

ISBN: 978-1-78097-274-9

Editor: Martin Corteel
Editorial Assistant: David Ballheimer
Project Art Editor: Darren Jordan
Production: Janette Burgin

Printed and bound by CPI Group (UK) Ltd, Croydon, CR0 4YY

THE
TOUR DE FRANCE
MISCELLANY

JOHN WHITE

CARLTON

❋ INTRODUCTION ❋

Who would have thought that the first edition of a bike race in France in 1903 would become one of the most watched events in sport and one of the greatest tests of human endurance for an athlete in any sport? The Tour de France was the brainchild of Henri Desgrange who organised the race to help boost sales of his sports newspaper, *L'Auto* (predecessor of today's *L'Equipe*), which was struggling to match the sales of its main rival, *Le Vélo*. Indeed, when the participants in the inaugural Tour de France rode through the various towns and villages which made up the six stages many of the residents did not bother to watch them ride past their front door.

Today, the Tour de France is the single most watched sporting event in the world with millions lining the route of each stage to cheer on their favourite rider. And whereas the 1903 race comprised amateur participants from France, Belgium, Italy and Switzerland, the 2013 event, the 100th edition of the Tour de France, includes professional cyclists from all over the world. The 1903 Tour de France did not include any mountain passes whereas the modern-day edition of the race sees the riders race over the Alps and the Pyrenees and take in some legendary climbs such as the historic L'Alpe d'Huez. And it is in the mountains where many Tours are lost and won although recently the Tour winners are also very capable time-trial specialists.

The first Tour de France took 18 days to complete, with rest-days included, and started in from close to the Au Reveil Matin café in Bergeron, near Paris, on 1 July 1903. The subsequent stages began in Lyon, Marseille, Toulouse, Bordeaux and Nantes, before finishing in Paris on 18 July 1903, with the victor being a Frenchman, Maurice Garin. In the early years of the Tour, stages regularly took as long as 17 hours to complete, so riders would often set off on a stage in the early hours of the morning, around first light. In 2012, Bradley Wiggins became the first British cyclist to ride into Paris wearing the coveted race-leader's yellow jersey.

And so to the Centenary Tour de France in 2013, when the world will watch men push their bodies to the limit of physical exertion in pursuit of glory and the honour of standing on the top step of the podium on the famous Avenue des Champs-Elysées in Paris wearing the most famous winner's shirt in sport, the *maillot jaune*.

Vive Le Tour!

John White
Carryduff, Co. Down, January 2013

❋ THE TOUR IS BORN ❋

The magazine *L'Auto-Vélo* was launched in 1902 in a bid to force its rival, *Le Vélo*, out of business. *L'Auto-Vélo* was completely devoted to sport with a particular emphasis on cycling, and in contrast to its competitor's green paper was printed on yellow paper. Henri Desgrange, a cycling promoter and former racer, was appointed as *L'Auto-Vélo*'s first editor. In November 1902, Géo Lefèvre, who had left *Le Vélo* to cover cycling for *L'Auto* (it was forced to change its name following a lawsuit), suggested to Desgrange the idea of a race on the major roads across France. This was the beginning of the Tour de France with the first race taking place the following year in 1903.

❋ SPANISH HAT-TRICK IN THE TOUR ❋

In 2008, Carlos Sastre won his first Tour de France crown and became the third Spaniard in consecutive years to win the greatest cycle race in the world, following Oscar Pereiro in 2006 and Alberto Contador in 2007. Alberto Contador won his second overall *maillot jaune* in 2009, making it four Tour de France wins in succession for Spanish riders.

❋ BABY-FACED ASSASSINS ❋

In 1983 Laurent Fignon, aged 22, won the Tour de France and joined the exclusive club of riders who had won the Tour at their first attempt. The other maiden post-war Tour victors were Fausto Coppi (1949), Hugo Koblet (1951), Jacques Anquetil (1957), Felice Gimondi (1965), Eddy Merckx (1969) and Bernard Hinault (1978).

❋ POSITIVE DOPE TEST FOR TOUR WINNER ❋

Bernard Thévenet, winner of the 1977 Tour de France, was penalised for a positive dope test in the Paris–Nice stage race held in March 1977 prior to his Tour success.

❋ IRON MAN FROM THE USA ❋

The 1992 Tour de France saw the first appearance of the iron man of American cycling, Frankie Andreu (Motorola). Andreu went on to ride in and complete nine consecutive Tours.

❋ GREAT TOURS DE FRANCE (1): 1903 ❋

In the first Tour de France, there were only six stages, ranging from 268km (167 miles) to 471km (293 miles) and an overall distance of 2,428km (1,509 miles). Sixty riders (49 of them French) set off from Paris to Lyon on 1 July for the first stage, which was won by pre-race favourite Maurice Garin. In those days, riders who abandoned during a stage were allowed to resume from the next one. This explains why the winners of the second, third – Hippolyte Aucouturier – and fourth – Charles Laesser (the Swiss rider was also the first non-French winner) – stages were excluded from the overall classification. Garin won the last two stages and arrived back in Paris on 19 July almost three hours ahead of the next rider, Lucien Pothier.

Rank	Name	Country	Time
1.	Maurice Garin	France	94h 33' 14"
2.	Lucien Pothier	France	+2h 59' 21"
3.	Fernand Augereau	France	+4h 29' 24"
4.	Rodolfo Muller	Italy	+4h 39' 30"
5.	Jean Fischer	France	+4h 58' 44"
6.	Marcel Kerff	Belgium	+5h 52' 24"
7.	Julien Lootens	Belgium	+8h 31' 08"
8.	Georges Pasquier	France	+10h 24' 04"
9.	François Beaugendre	France	+10h 52' 14"
10.	Aloïs Catteau	France	+12h 44' 57"

Did You Know That?
Road works outside the offices of *L'Auto* newspaper meant the starting point of the first Tour de France had to be moved a few hundred metres to the Au Reveil Matin café.

❋ TOUR SPOKESMEN (1) ❋

"You are murderers!"
Octave Lapize to Tour organisers after an Alpine stage in 1911

❋ FIRST FOREIGN TOUR ❋

In 1954 the Tour de France saw the first foreign start in its 51-year history. The anticlockwise Tour (it visited the Pyrenees first) set off from Amsterdam, with the first stage finishing in Beveren, Belgium. The winner of the Tour's inaugural foreign start was Wout Wagtmans (Belgium).

✳ DIZZY HEIGHTS ✳

In 2010 the Tour celebrated the 100th anniversary of climbing in the Pyrenees, while in 2011, 100 years of riding in the Alps was celebrated by including the highest-ever stage finish in the history of the race. Three massive cols faced the riders: the Agnel, which was being ridden for the first time ever from this side, the Izoard with its legendary Casse Déserte, and the Galibier. The Col du Galibier, which was first crossed in 1911 and is the most visited mountain pass in the Tour's history, was visited twice during the 2011 race. Stage 18 was the first time the peloton finished on the 2,645-metre (8,678 feet) Alpine pass, thereby making it the highest summit finish in Tour history, beating that of the Col du Granon (2,413 metres (7,917 feet) during the 1986 Tour de France.

✳ UCI WORLD RANKINGS ✳

In March 1984 the Union Cycliste Internationale (UCI) introduced a system of world rankings for the first time. Sean Kelly (Ireland) was the first rider to be ranked world number one and was the year-end rankings leader for six years from 1984 to 1989 inclusive. Only Laurent Jalabert (France) has come close to matching Kelly's record six years as No.1 by surpassing his peers from 1995–1997 and then for a fourth time in 1999.

✳ CYCLING'S RUGBY CONNECTION ✳

The traditional final stage finish on the Champs-Elysées during the 2007 Tour de France started in Marcoussis, the home of the French rugby union team's training camp. France was the host nation of the 2007 Rugby Union World Cup.

✳ THE MAGNIFICENT SEVEN IN THE GC ✳

Laurent Fignon's System U squad won Stage 2 of the 1986 Tour de France, a 56-kilometre team time trial, resulting in System U riders occupying the top seven places in the GC (general classification).

✳ BELGIAN STAGE DROUGHT ✳

The 2002 Tour de France failed to see a Belgian stage winner for the first time since 1997, while Axel Merckx – Eddy's son – was the Tour's highest ranked Belgian, finishing 28th in the general classification.

✹ TOUR LEGENDS (1) – FAUSTO COPPI ✹

Angelo Fausto Coppi was born on 15 September 1919 in Castellania, a small village near Liguria, Italy. One of five children, he was a delivery boy for the local butcher and delivering meat allowed him to meet and befriend the famous blind masseur, Biagio Cavanna. The pair bonded immediately and Cavanna agreed to train the young Coppi, who possessed an almost inhuman heartbeat of 30–40 times per minute. Coppi entered his first cycling race in July 1937, a road race on the local Boffalora circuit. The following year, Fausto won his first race at Castelletto d'Orba wearing the white and sky-blue jersey for which he became famous.

The outbreak of the Second World War deprived cycling fans of Coppi's undoubted brilliance and, when the hostilities ended, Italy needed sporting heroes to help lift the mood of the nation. Italy was blessed with two cyclists who fitted the bill: Coppi and Gino Bartali, who won the Giro d'Italia (Italy's version of the Tour de France) in 1936, 1937 and 1946 and the Tour de France in 1938 and 1948.

In 1946, Coppi achieved one of his greatest victories in the Milan–San Remo race. Three miles (5km) into the 181-mile (292km) event, Coppi and nine other riders attacked, but Fausto dropped all his rivals on the climb up the Turchino and went on to win by 14 minutes.

In 1949, Coppi won the Giro d'Italia, then stole Bartali's crown – in this case his *maillot jaune* – and thus became the first cyclist to complete the Giro–Tour de France double. He dominated the Tour, taking the overall classification and the King of the Mountains prize. Three years later, he repeated all three triumphs and, in 1950, completed a different double, taking the Giro d'Italia and the World Championship Road Race. In addition to his victories in the Giro d'Italia and Tour de France, Fausto also won three out of five of cycling's monuments (these are the Paris–Roubaix, Milan–San Remo, Tour of Flanders, Liège–Bastogne–Liège and Giro di Lombardia races), achieving nine victories overall.

He was a master tactician, whether the stage was over a climb, a long distance or a sprint finish. Among his 138 road races wins were two Tours de France, five each of the Giro d'Italia and Giro di Lombardia – both records – and three Milan–San Remo; he also won 84 out of 95 track pursuit races.

Tragically, Fausto lost his brother Serse, who died after a crash in a sprint finish in the Giro del Piemonte in 1951. He also died very young, on 2 January 1960 aged just 40, from malaria, following a hunting safari to Africa.

Did You Know That?
Fausto Coppi was nicknamed *Il Campionissimo* – "the Champion of Champions" – by his home fans.

✳ TOUR SCANDALS (1) ✳

During the 1967 Tour de France Britain's Tom Simpson died from heart failure on the ascent of Mont Ventoux. After traces of amphetamines were found in his bloodstream, the sport's governing body introduced doping tests the following year.

✳ TOUR AND PARIS–ROUBAIX DOUBLE ✳

In 1910, Octave Lapize became the first rider to win the Tour de France and Paris–Roubaix race in the same year. Maurice Garin, winner of the inaugural Tour in 1903, had previously won the Paris–Roubaix in both 1897 and 1898. The famous Paris–Roubaix race was first held in 1896 when Josef Fischer (Germany) mastered the cobblestones. Roubaix is in north-eastern France, not far from Lille and very close to the border with Belgium.

✳ TOUR SPOKESMEN (2) ✳

"As long as I live and breathe, I attack."
Five-time Tour winner Bernard Hinault

✳ TOUR WINNER DIES IN THE GREAT WAR ✳

Lucien Petit-Breton was the first rider to win the Tour de France twice, doing so in consecutive years (1907 and 1908). During the First World War, Petit-Breton was a driver in the French army and was killed in a head-on collision.

✳ BIG MEN UPSTAGED ✳

In Stage 2 of the 1931 Tour de France Henri Desgrange decided that the *touriste-routiers* would start the stage ten minutes after the national teams. However rather than deter the non-sponsored riders, it merely drove them on. Max Bulla, a *touriste-routier*, not only caught the starters but also won the stage and took the overall lead. Bulla has the distinction of being the first and only *touriste-routier* to wear the famous yellow jersey in a Tour de France.

✳ A HELPING HAND BANNED ✳

Léon Scieur was having a bad day on Stage 3 of the 1919 Tour de France, suffering four flat tyres on his way to Brest. During one of his enforced stops he took cover from the heavy rain in a doorway to carry out repairs. Alongside him was the lady who lived in the house as well as one of Henri Desgrange's race commissars, who kept a watchful eye over Scieur to ensure he received no assistance from the lady. This was at a time when the rules strictly forbade a rider from receiving any form of help. After a while Scieur's fingers became too cold to even thread the needle he used to re-sew the tubulars and so Scieur asked the lady to thread the needle for him. However, the race commissar informed him that if she threaded the needle he would receive a time penalty.

✳ SNAIL'S PACE ✳

With an average speed of 33.407 kilometres an hour, the 1973 Tour de France was the slowest since Louison Bobet's 1954 victory.

✳ YELLOW JERSEY CRASHES OUT ✳

Stage 2 of the 1991 Tour de France was a team time trial, and Rolf Sorensen's Ariostea squad won the stage which put Sorensen in the yellow jersey. The Dane retained the yellow jersey until Stage 5, when he hit a traffic island and broke his clavicle four kilometres from the finish line. His Tour was over.

✳ A RED-HOT FAVOURITE ✳

Eddy Merckx (Molteni), the five times Tour de France winner, went into the 1975 Tour in outstanding form. Not only was he defending his yellow jersey win in 1974, he was also the reigning World Road Champion and had won Milan–San Remo, Amstel Gold, the Tour of Flanders and Liège–Bastogne–Liège. He also claimed victory in the Catalonian Week and the Tour of Sardinia and was second in Paris–Nice (to Joop Zoetemelk), second in Paris–Roubaix (to Roger De Vlaeminck) and second in the Tour of Switzerland (losing to Roger De Vlaeminck by 55 seconds). The Belgian master was out to claim his sixth Tour title and surpass his own and Jacques Anquetil's record of five Tour wins. However, the red-hot favourite finished second to Bernard Thévenet (Peugeot-BP) at 2 minutes 47 seconds.

✻ PUT ME BACK ON MY BIKE ✻

Many people have read that the last words spoken by Tom Simpson prior to his death on the ascent of Mount Ventoux in the 13th stage of the 1967 Tour de France were: "Put me back on my bike." However, in Owen Mulholland's *Uphill Battle: Cycling's Great Climbers* we learn that when Simpson fell the first time, he told the British team mechanic Harry Hall: "Get me up, get me up. I want to go on. Get me up, get me straight." The following day the peloton sought and obtained the Tour organisers' permission for one of Simpson's British teammates to claim a ceremonial stage victory to honour Simpson's memory. All the teams rode slowly and allowed Barry Hoban to cross the finish line alone.

✻ MOUNTAINOUS CHANGES ✻

In 1928 Henri Desgrange changed the route of the first Pyrenean stage of the Tour de France from the one he had adopted since 1913. Consequently instead of the normal Bayonne to Luchon route he started the stage at Hendaye, crossing the Aubisque and the Tourmalet, before arriving at Luchon. The Aspin and the Peyresourde were not included in the route.

✻ *LA FRANÇAISE* COLLAPSE AGAIN ✻

In 1913 the *La Française* team in the Tour de France had some outstanding riders, including Maurice Brocco, Paul Duboc, Emile Georget and Octave Lapize. With the Tour now reverting to an elapsed time method of calculating the winner, it was quite a formidable team. However as it transpired, none of the eight men on the *La Française* team made it to the fifth stage. This was the second year in succession that the team abandoned the race.

✻ CHIMNEY SWEEP CLEANS UP ✻

On 19 July 1903, 21 of the 60 riders who began the inaugural Tour de France crossed the finish line in front of 20,000 spectators at Paris's Parc des Princes velodrome. The race leader Maurice Garin, riding the red, white and blue tricolour bike of his sponsor, *La Française*, won the final stage and with it overall victory. Garin was nicknamed "The Chimney-Sweep" after his occupation before he became a professional cyclist. Amazingly, the final finisher came in more than two days later.

❋ GREAT CLIMBS (1) – L'ALPE D'HUEZ ❋

L'Alpe d'Huez was first visited in 1952, and it would be 24 more years before riders again faced the 21 hairpin bends to the summit. Since then, the Alpe d'Huez has become a Tour staple and the 100th edition in 2013 included two separate climbs in the same stage. A stage-winner is commemorated by a plaque on a bend and, having gone from 21 to 1 by 1999, Tour organisers have gone back to bend 21 for subsequent winners. Only two Frenchmen have won stages (Bernard Hinault and Pierre Rolland), but three Dutchmen (Peter Winnen, Joop Zoetemelk and Hennie Kuiper) have won twice.

Location: The département of Isère and in the Rhônes-Alpes region of SE France.

Nearest town: Huez.

Height: The peak is 3,330m, but the stage finish is at 1,860m.

Gradient: From Bourg d'Oisans, the ascent is 1,071m over 13.2km, with an average gradient of 8.1 percent, but the first 1.5km has an average gradient of 10.4 percent.

Characteristics: The road up to the finish traverses 21 hairpin bends, which enables up to 300,000 fans to line the route.

Tour visits: 27 in total (two stages in 1979 and 2013, and an individual time trial in 2004). It has always been a stage finish.

Multiple winners: 2 wins: Hennie Kuiper (1977, 1978), Joop Zoetemelk (1976, 1979 2nd climb), Peter Winnen (1981, 1983), Gianni Bugno (1990, 1991), Marco Pantani (1995, 1997), No winner* (2001, 2004).

Conquerors of the peak – one-time winners: Fausto Coppi (1952), Joaquin Agostinho (1979, first climb), Beat Breu (1982), Luis Herrera (1984), Bernard Hinault (1986), Federico Echave (1987), Steve Rooks (1988), Gert-Jan Theunisse (1989), Andrew Hampsten (1992), Roberto Conti (1994), Giuseppe Guerini (1999), Iban Mayo (2003), Frank Schleck (2006), Carlos Sastre (2008), Pierre Rolland (2011).

** = Lance Armstrong won in 2001 and 2004 but, in 2012, he was stripped of all his stage wins.*

Did You Know That?
The first year that motorcycle television crews followed the Tour was in 1952 – the same year L'Alpe d'Huez made its debut – and Italian Fausto Coppi's breakaway from Jean Robic 6m from the end of the stage made him a Tour legend.

✳ ITALIAN ROAD FORCE ✳

The Italians entered a superb team in the 1938 Tour de France with Gino Bartali (1936 and 1937 Giro d'Italia winner), Vasco Bergamaschi (1935 Giro d'Italia winner), Aldo Bini, Giuseppe Martano, Jules Rossi and Mario Vicini (runner-up in the 1937 Tour). Bartali won the first of his two Tour de France victories in 1938.

✳ THE PEDALLING MADMAN ✳

In 1950 Ferdy Kübler became the first Swiss rider to win the Tour de France. Kübler was known variously as "The Pedalling Madman" because of his demonic grin or as "The Eagle of Adilswil" after the Swiss village where he grew up. In 1951, Kübler won the World Championship, Liège–Bastogne–Liège, the Flèche Wallonne, and the Tours of Romandie and Switzerland. He also came in third in the Giro d'Italia but surprisingly he did not attempt to retain his Tour de France title in 1951. It has been suggested that Kübler declined the offer to ride on the Swiss team in the 1951 Tour de France because he would have had to play a support role to his fellow countryman and rival, Hugo Koblet.

✳ TOUR SPOKESMEN (3) ✳

"I'm going to do my best to defend my dignity and my innocence." *Floyd Landis, original 2006 Tour de France winner, after receiving the news that he tested positive for an abnormal testosterone-to-epitestosterone level*

✳ THREE-WAY SPLIT ✳

Stage 1 of the 1971 Tour de France was a gruelling three-split ordeal. The first, a 62-kilometre ride to Basel in Switzerland, ended with all 130 riders finishing together. The three-stage schedule was so hectic that some of the riders had not crossed the finish line of the second split by the time the third split was starting.

✻ FRENCH TOUR WINNERS ✻

1	5 wins	Jacques Anquetil	(1957, 1961, 1962, 1963, 1964)
=	5 wins	Bernard Hinault	(1978, 1979, 1981, 1982, 1985)
3	3 wins	Louison Bobet	(1953, 1954, 1955)
4	2 wins	Lucien Petit-Breton	(1907, 1908)
=	2 wins	André Leducq	(1930, 1932)
=	2 wins	Antonin Magne	(1931, 1934)
=	2 wins	Bernard Thévenet	(1975, 1977)
=	2 wins	Laurent Fignon	(1983, 1984)
9	1 win	Maurice Garin	(1903)
=	1 win	Henri Cornet	(1904)
=	1 win	Louis Trousselier	(1905)
=	1 win	René Pottier	(1906)
=	1 win	Octave Lapize	(1910)
=	1 win	Gustave Garrigou	(1911)
=	1 win	Henri Pélissier	(1923)
=	1 win	Georges Speicher	(1933)
=	1 win	Roger Lapébie	(1937)
=	1 win	Jean Robic	(1947)
=	1 win	Roger Walkowiak	(1956)
=	1 win	Lucien Aimar	(1966)
=	1 win	Roger Pingeon	(1967)

✻ GLORIOUS COMEBACK DENIED ✻

Chris Boardman, who broke his ankle in the opening prologue of the 1995 Tour de France, came within two seconds of taking the leader's yellow jersey in the opening prologue of the 1996 Tour. Alex Zulle of Switzerland, second overall in the 1995 Tour, deprived the British Olympic pursuit champion of a glorious comeback. It was the second time the 28-year-old Swiss rider pulled on the famous *maillot jaune*, having had it for a day in the 1992 Tour.

✻ FRANCE'S TOUR DE FORCE ✻

Many Tour de France writers down the years consider the 1933 French team as the finest collection of pre-war riders to compete in the race. They had the two times winner André Leducq (1930 and 1932), Antonin Magne (1931 winner) and future winners Georges Speicher (1933) and Roger Lapébie (1937). In addition to the champions/future champions they had Maurice Archambaud, Léon LeCalvez, René Le Grevès and the king of sprinters, Charles Pélissier.

✳ TOUR SPOKESMEN (4) ✳

"I won't start my preparation right away for next year's Tour. I want to take some time off but I'll be back next year to win, I'm not looking for second place!"
Lance Armstrong in 2003

✳ PARIS SNUBBED AGAIN ✳

In 1951 the Tour de France headed inland for the first time to the Massif Central, crossed Mont Ventoux and, unusually, started outside Paris – unusually because this was only the second time since the inaugural Tour in 1903 that the race had not started in Paris.

✳ GRAND PRIX DES NATIONS ✳

During the early 1930s the evening newspaper, *Paris-Soir*, the main rival to Henri Desgrange's *L'Auto* (a morning paper), reported the details of the day's stage of the Tour de France in full that evening whereas *L'Auto* effectively reported old news the next day. In order to make its deadline, the reporters from *Paris-Soir* would write a few pages at a time as the stage progressed and then hand them to a colleague to telephone through to Head Office. However, the quick-thinking Desgrange decided to start the stages much later in the day so that when the winner crossed the stage finish line it was well past the deadline required by *Paris-Soir*. Not to be outdone, *Paris-Soir* and its sports editor Gaston Bénac followed a familiar route and decided to host their own bicycle race to rival the Tour de France. Bénac's creation was the *Grand Prix des Nations*, a time trial that eventually became the unofficial world championship of time trialling. Bénac's first *Grand Prix des Nations* was staged in 1932 and was not universally accepted by the professional riders. Indeed Bénac had trouble convincing them to participate because at the time trialling was not as popular as it is today. The first *Grand Prix des Nations* was won by Maurice Archambaud.

✳ HISTORY MAKER ✳

In 1949, Fausto Coppi (Italy) did something that no other professional cyclist had ever done before: having won the Giro d'Italia, he went on to win the Tour de France in the same year at his first attempt.

A QUAD OF OPENING STAGE WINS

In 1959, André Darrigade (France) won the first stage and the first yellow jersey for the fourth successive year in the Tour de France.

THE *MAILLOT VERT*

The *maillot vert* (green jersey) is worn by the leader of the points classification in the Tour. It was first introduced in 1953 and while the yellow jersey is awarded for the lowest cumulative time in the race, the green jersey is awarded for the points won by a rider during each stage and at intermediate "hot spots". The green jersey has been sponsored by PMU for more than 10 years.

THE FLYING FRENCHMAN

When Lucien Petit-Breton (France) won the 1907 Tour de France he became the first rider to have both held the World Hour Record and won an overall yellow jersey. Petit-Breton set his World Hour Record (41.110 km/h) on 24 August 1905 on the Buffalo cycling track in Paris and lost it to Marcel Berthet (France) on 20 June 1907 (41.520 km/h).

BOBET TREBLE

Louison Bobet (France) went into the 1955 Tour de France looking for his third consecutive overall *maillot jaune* victory. Bobet was in exceptional form entering the 1955 Tour because not only was he reigning World Road Champion, but during the spring he also won the Tour of Flanders, he was third in Paris–Roubaix, he won the Dauphiné Libéré and he was runner-up to André Darrigade in the French road championships. Assisted by a strong team comprising his brother Jean, Jean Dotto, Jean Forestier, Raphaël Géminiani, Jean Malléjac, Antonin Rolland and André Darrigade, Bobet won his third Tour de France.

CHIAPPUCCI'S GRAND TOURS

The flamboyant Italian rider Claudio Chiappucci's Grand Tour accomplishments are impressive: Tour de France: 2nd twice, 3rd place and a King of the Mountains jersey. For the Giro d'Italia: 2nd twice, 3rd, 4th, 5th, plus two King of the Mountains jerseys and one Points jersey.

✳ THE PUBLICITY CARAVAN ✳

In the 1930 Tour de France, Henri Desgrange introduced a system of national and regional teams in place of trade teams, which he openly hated: competitors would now ride for France, Italy, Spain and other countries and the riders were required to use identical yellow, anonymous bikes. Although the public warmed to the idea, the team sponsors complained that they had lost much needed publicity from the sport's most prestigious race and furthermore, they still had to pay the riders' wages. Desgrange was now faced with a huge bill for the expenses of running the teams during the Tour including transportation, food and lodging. On top of this he feared that the bicycle manufacturers would withdraw their advertising from his newspaper and Tour sponsor, *L'Auto*. But Desgrange, who was always looking to maximise publicity for his race, invented the sponsors' caravan whereby companies could pay a fee to follow the race with cars and vans bearing their logo and advertising their products. The chocolate manufacturer Menier was the first company to sign up to Desgrange's new idea, and only two more joined the publicity caravan in the first year.

✳ TEAM TIME TRIALS THAT MATTER ✳

The 1979 Tour de France had five individual time trials totalling 165.3 kilometres and two team time trials covering a colossal 176.8 kilometres. In previous Tours team time trials had counted only towards the team classification, but in this edition of the Tour the team's real time in the stage counted towards the individual rider's elapsed time.

✳ DESGRANGE STEPS DOWN ✳

From the inaugural Tour de France in 1903 until the 1935 race, Henri Desgrange had been in charge of all of them. However a few weeks prior to the 1936 Tour, Desgrange, now 71 years old, needed kidney surgery. Undeterred by his condition he had a car fitted with cushions to ease his pain and set off with the riders on Stage 1. By the end of the second stage, Desgrange knew he couldn't continue and handed the management of the race to Jacques Goddet, the son of Victor Goddet, the financial controller of *L'Auto* who had supported Desgrange in organising the inaugural race. On 16 August 1940, his health having continued to deteriorate, Henri Desgrange, Father of the Tour de France, died in his house on the French Riviera.

❋ THE 1923 AUTOMOTO TEAM ❋

The Automoto Team that took part in the 1923 Tour de France included some outstanding riders: Henri Pélissier (1923 Tour winner), Francis Pélissier, Honoré Barthélémy, Hector Heusghem, Victor Lenaers and future Tour winner Lucien Buysse (1926). In support of their Italian commercial interests they also signed Ottavio Bottecchia (Italy), who had turned professional the previous year and finished fifth in the Giro d'Italia just two weeks earlier. Automoto also hired Alphonse Baugé, who had in previous Tours guided Alcyon and Peugeot to victory, to manage the team.

❋ CHAMPION UNABLE TO DEFEND TOUR ❋

In 1939 the Italian Gino Bartali was prevented from defending the Tour de France he had won in 1938 because of the conflict that continued to fester in Europe. As well as Italy, Spain and Germany declined to send teams to the 1939 Tour. Roger Lapébie, the 1937 Tour winner, was injured and couldn't ride, while Tour greats André Leducq and Antonin Magne had ridden their last Tour the previous year. Sylvère Maes from the Belgian "A" team, winner of the Tour in 1936, won the 1939 Tour de France.

❋ NOT A SURPRISE WINNER ❋

Gustave Garrigou's (France, Alcyon) victory in the 1911 Tour de France was no surprise. Here are some of his achievements leading up to his yellow jersey triumph:

    1907: French Champion, Tour of Lombardy, second in the
           Tour de France
    1908: French Champion, fourth in the Tour de France
    1909: Second in the Tour de France

He won two stages in the 1911 Tour and also won Milan–San Remo. Garrigou went on to get a second, a third and a fifth in the Tour before the First World War ended his career as a professional rider.

❋ TOUR WINNER NOT HUMAN ❋

Hugo Koblet won the 1951 Tour de France by 22 minutes from Raphaël Géminiani. Géminiani joked, "Chasing after these white crosses (the Swiss national jersey), you could end up finishing at the Red Cross!" Géminiani claimed to be the real winner. When asked about Koblet, he replied, "He doesn't count. I'm the first human."

❋ MOUNTAIN KINGS ❋

Up to and including the win by Thomas Voeckler (France, Team Europcar) in the 2012 Tour, France has had the highest number of King of the Mountains winners with 21, followed by Spain (17), Italy (11), Belgium (11), Colombia (4), Denmark (2), Luxembourg (2), Netherlands (2), Switzerland (1) and the United Kingdom (1). Richard Virenque (France) holds the record for the highest number of King of the Mountains titles with an incredible seven (1994–97, 1999, 2003–04).

❋ ANQUETIL MONUMENTS ❋

There is a large black monument situated beside the traffic lights near the church in the village of Quincampoix, north of Rouen, where Jacques Anquetil is buried. The monument lists all of Anquetil's achievements. Another monument in honour of Anquetil, who was born in Mont-Saint-Aigan, near Rouen, stands at the Piste Municipale track in Paris, where the centre is named after him.

❋ TOUR SPOKESMEN (5) ❋

"I have no doubt I have the engine to come back. It's just a matter of working well and doing the right things. I need to be patient ... I think you gain shape quicker than what you lose it."

Andy Schleck, who missed the 2012 Tour because of an injury

❋ FROM RIDER TO SPONSOR ❋

After he retired from racing in 1960 Raphaël Géminiani, a former Tour de France rider, started to equip professional cycling teams to promote his own bikes, which were made for him by Mercier and other firms. Géminiani obtained the backing of aperitif makers St Raphaël for his own team, which at that time had Jacques Anquetil on its roster. The 1962 St Raphaël team is widely regarded as the first professional team to be financed mainly by a firm outside the cycling industry.

❋ THE THREE PEAKS ❋

Along with the Tour de France and the World Cycling Championship, the Giro d'Italia makes up the Triple Crown of Cycling.

❋ DOG DAY AFTERNOON ❋

Luis Ocaña, winner of the 1973 Tour de France, had an inauspicious start to the race when a dog ran in front of him just 10 kilometres into the afternoon's half-stage on the opening day. Ocaña and Herman van Springel crashed to the ground but managed to remount and continue racing. Van Springel finished runner-up in the stage to Jose Catieau, one of Ocaña's *domestiques*, but claimed the yellow jersey.

❋ THE BADGER RETURNS ❋

After abandoning the 1980 Tour de France as a result of tendonitis in his knee following Stage 12, Bernard Hinault went into the 1981 Tour looking for his third win. He was in absolutely superb form and although he did not attempt to defend his 1980 Giro d'Italia victory he was still the reigning World Champion, and had won Paris–Roubaix, the Amstel Gold race, the Criterium International and the Dauphiné Libéré. Hinault achieved his goal for 1981 by winning the Tour at 14 minutes 34 seconds over the 1976 winner Lucien van Impe.

❋ EARLY TOUR HOOLIGANISM ❋

The 1904 Tour de France was plagued with factional hooliganism. When fans learned that the winner of the inaugural 1903 Tour, Maurice Garin (France), was receiving food from a race official, they were outraged. It was against the rules for riders to receive assistance from anyone, let alone a race official. During Stage 2, on the Col de la République, a gang hid in wait for the riders; they planned on beating up or even stabbing the leaders to help local favourite, Antoine Faure. When Garin and Giovanni Gerbi (Italy) reached the mob, they were attacked. Gerbi suffered broken fingers and was forced to return to Italy, while Garin managed to escape unhurt after race officials intervened. In Stage 3, Ferdinand Payan was disqualified for taking pace from riders who weren't even entered in the race. When the Tour went through Nîmes, close to Payan's home town of Alès, there was another riot. The riders were forced to defend themselves in a fight with Payan's fans, who had travelled from Alès to obstruct the race. When it was discovered that some of the mob were armed with weapons, a Tour official had to fire a revolver to disperse the crowd. Meanwhile, nails were thrown on to the roads all along the 1904 Tour route.

❋ GREAT TOURS DE FRANCE (2): 1910 ❋

A major new wrinkle was added to the eighth edition of the Tour de France: the high mountains. *L'Auto* journalist Adolphe Steines was despatched to the Pyrenees to discover if the mountains were viable. The answer was in the positive, so the riders were faced with the Portet d'Aspet (on Stage 9), Col de Peyresourde, Col d'Aspin, Col du Tourmalet and, lastly, the Col d'Aubisque (all on Stage 10). It was a gruelling Tour, covering 4,737km (2,943 miles), and only 41 of 110 riders were able to make it back to Paris, with Octave Lapize, a noted climber, topping the overall classification. As he completed Stage 10, he famously screamed at the organisers, "You are murderers, yes murderers!"

Rank	Name	Country	Points
1.	Octave Lapize	France	63
2.	François Faber	Luxembourg	67
3.	Gustave Garrigou	France	86
4.	Cyrille van Hauwaert	Belgium	97
5.	Charles Cruchon	France	119
6.	Charles Crupelandt	France	148
7.	Ernest Paul	France	154
8.	André Blaise	France	166
9.	Julien Maitron	France	171
10.	Aldo Bettini	Italy	175

Did You Know That?
The 1910 Tour, as well as being the first to venture into the High Mountains, was also the first to have *la voiture-balai*, the "broom wagon" which swept up the last finisher of a stage or a rider who abandoned the Tour.

❋ TOUR SPOKESMEN (6) ❋

"If it takes ten to kill me, I'll take nine and win."
Tom Simpson

❋ DOUBLE HAT-TRICK FOR ZABEL ❋

In 1998, Erik Zabel (Germany) claimed his third consecutive overall green sprinters' jersey victory in the Tour de France. He then went on to achieve a second hat-trick of points classification victories in the Tour de France by winning the *maillot vert* in 1999, 2000 and 2001. No rider has won more overall green jerseys than Zabel.

✻ TOUR LEGENDS (2) – LOUISON BOBET ✻

Louis "Louison" Bobet was born on 12 March 1925 in Saint-Méen-le-Grand, near Rennes, France. His father was a baker, also named Louis, so he was given the nickname *Louison*, "Little Louis". Louison was just two years old when his father bought him his first bicycle, and although a talented all-round sportsman, his uncle Raymond told him he could become a professional racer. At the age of 13, Bobet rode in his first competitive race, and finished second in a sprint finish at the end of a 19-mile (30km) course.

Bobet served in the army during the Second World War but, after demobilisation in December 1945, he applied for a racing cyclist's licence and was mistakenly sent one for a semi-professional. In 1947, he turned professional and entered the Tour de France for the first time. However, he abandoned the race after just nine days, beaten by the Alps.

His second attempt was much more successful and he won two stages, finishing fourth in the overall classification. In 1949, he pulled out after the first day in the mountains, but rebounded in 1950, not only winning the French national road racing championship but also achieving a third-place finish in the Tour de France, including two stage wins and the King of the Mountains title. Louison retained his national title in 1951, but had a disappointing Tour, finishing a lowly 20th after another bad spell in the mountains. However, he displayed his climbing talent by winning the mountains classification in that year's Giro d'Italia.

After missing the 1952 Tour, Bobet was spectacular in 1953, finishing second in the King of the Mountain competition, winning two more stages and the overall classification for the first time. He retained his *maillot jaune* the following year, adding another three stage wins. In 1955, Louison became the first rider to win the Tour de France in three consecutive years (again winning two stages), despite suffering from an agonising saddle boil for most of the race.

Bobet took a few years out from racing, but returned to the saddle in 1958 and finished seventh in the Tour de France general classification. His last Tour was in 1959, but he abandoned following Stage 18.

It wasn't just the grand tours at which Louison excelled. He also won the Milan–San Remo Classic in 1951, the Tour of Lombardy Classic in 1951, the World Championship Road Race in 1954 (he was second in 1957 and 1958), the Tour of Flanders Classic in 1955 and the Paris–Roubaix Classic in 1956.

He died from cancer on 13 March 1983, aged 58.

Did You Know That?
Jean Bobet – Louison's brother – finished 14th overall in the 1955 Tour de France and 15th overall two years later.

❋ HE RODE A WOMAN'S BIKE ❋

In 1928, Nicolas Frantz (Alcyon) won his second successive Tour de France. In Stage 19, from Metz to Charleville, the frame of Frantz's bicycle broke as he rode across a railway crossing with 100km of the race still to go. However Frantz, who was leading the Tour, borrowed an undersized, woman's bicycle complete with wide saddle, fenders, and bell to finish the stage and retain his yellow jersey.

❋ TURKEY SHOOT ❋

On 20 April 1987, Greg LeMond was out turkey hunting with his brother-in-law who accidentally shot him. A total of 40 shotgun pellets ripped into the reigning Tour de France champion's body, resulting in the loss of three-quarters of his blood and the collapse of his right lung. Around 30 pellets could not be removed because of their location, including some in his heart lining, liver, small intestine and diaphragm. Needless to say, LeMond was unable to defend his *maillot jaune* in the 1987 Tour de France.

❋ DEBUTANT CLAIMS FIRST STAGE VICTORY ❋

In 1953, André Darrigade, from Narosse, France, in his maiden Tour de France, won Stage 12. In his career, Darrigade claimed 22 stage victories and twice won the Tour de France Points classification. He is considered one of the greatest French sprinters of all time.

❋ ANQUETIL FIRST TO FOUR ❋

Going into the 1963 Tour de France Jacques Anquetil, looking for his third consecutive Tour victory and his fourth overall winner's *maillot jaune*, was in scintillating form. In the spring he easily won Paris–Nice, the Dauphiné Libéré, the Criterium National and the Vuelta. In the Vuelta, in which he had been disappointed the previous year, he claimed victory in the same manner in which he won the 1961 Tour de France by taking the lead in the GC after the Stage 1b time trial on the opening day and never relinquishing the lead. Anquetil won the 1963 Tour, thereby becoming the first rider in the history of the race to win it four times.

✳ MERCKX CATCHES ANQUETIL ✳

Eddy Merckx entered the 1974 Tour de France in sparkling form, having won both the Giro d'Italia and the Tour of Switzerland. However his main challengers sensed that "The Cannibal" was losing his appetite for the fight because for the first time since he had turned professional in 1965, Merckx failed to claim victory in any of the Spring Classics. Nevertheless the cycling machine won the 1974 Tour to equal Jacques Anquetil's feat of five wins, and then went on to add the World Road Championship in 1974.

✳ COUNT ME OUT ✳

Philippe Thys (the winner in 1913, 1914, 1920) and Henri Pélissier (who won in 1923) both abandoned the 1925 Tour de France. Pélissier quit on Stage 4, while Thys bailed out on Stage 9 (Pélissier's brother, Francis, also quit on Stage 9).

✳ TOUR SPOKESMEN (7) ✳

"I used to work in a bank when I was younger and to me it doesn't matter whether it's raining or the sun is shining or whatever: as long as I'm riding a bike I know I'm the luckiest guy in the world."
Mark Cavendish, British cyclist, multiple stage winner of the Tour de France

✳ ANYONE FOR ICE-CREAM? ✳

Stage 18 of the 1954 Tour de France took the riders into the Alps with the Romeyere the first major climb of the first day. Spain's Federico Bahamontes, making his Tour debut, was first to the top of the mountain and when the chasing pack reached the summit they found Bahamontes sitting on a wall eating an ice-cream given to him by a spectator. The young Spaniard had a fear of descending and felt safer when he had others around him to help guide him down the mountain. Bahamontes finished the day 49th overall, 10 minutes behind the stage winner, but went on to win the climbers' competition in the Tour.

✳ STAGELESS CHAMPION ✳

Greg LeMond won the Tour de France in 1990 without claiming a stage victory. It was the American's third overall *maillot jaune* success.

❋ THE PENNINE WAY ❋

The 2014 Tour de France *grand départ* will be in Yorkshire, England, and the riders will then visit London before crossing over to France.

❋ A PELOTON WITHOUT A CHAMPION ❋

In the 1927 Tour de France, the previous year's winner, Lucien Buysse, chose not to defend his yellow jersey. Ottavio Bottecchia, winner in 1924 and 1925, had been found murdered two weeks before the start of the race. As a result this was the first Tour de France since the inaugural Tour in 1903 to start without a previous winner in the peloton.

❋ BROTHERS UP IN ARMS ❋

After finishing Stage 3 of the 1919 Tour de France alongside his brother Francis who won the stage, Henri Pélissier likened himself to a thoroughbred while the other riders were merely pack horses. Pélissier went on to say that he felt shorter stages at higher average speeds was what the Tour needed to grasp the public's attention. However, race organiser and Tour de France founder Henri Desgrange took exception to Pélissier's comments, and made fun of him in his magazine, *L'Auto*. The Pélissier brothers then withdrew from the race. This marked the beginning of a long-standing feud between two of the biggest personalities in cycling at the time, and it was not the first time the fiery brothers would quit the Tour.

❋ RIDER HIT BY HIS OWN CAR ❋

The 1995 Tour de France began in Brittany with a 7.4km prologue time trial held in the evening. For the first riders out the streets were dry, but as it began to rain the roads became slippery. The previous year's prologue winner, Chris Boardman, crashed heavily and was then hit by his own follow car. Boardman broke his ankle and wrist, thereby ending his Tour almost before it even began.

❋ WHEN IRISH EYES ARE SMILING ❋

Seamus Elliot, a member of Jacques Anquetil's St Raphaël team, won Stage 3 of the 1963 Tour to become the first Irishman in Tour de France history to wear the yellow jersey.

❀ GREAT CLIMBS (2) – COL D'AUBISQUE ❀

The Col d'Aubisque is a staple of the Tour de France, with the summit being crossed on 69 Tours (most recently in 2012 when Thomas Voeckler won the stage), and twice each in 1914 and 1985. Adolphe Steines, a journalist colleague of Tour founder Henri Desgrange, visited the Pyrenees in 1910 as the Tour went into the high mountains for the first time and he met the local official responsible for roads and bridges in that part of the Pyrenees. Asked about a stage climbing the Col, he said to Steines, "Take the riders up the Aubisque? You're completely crazy in Paris."

Location: The département of Pyrénées-Atlantique and region of Aquitaine, close to the France/Andorra/Spain border.

Nearest town: Tarbes.

Height: The Col d'Aubisque is a pass on the 2,613m Pic de Ger, peaking at 1,709m.

Gradient: There is one route from the west, starting at Laruns, which is a 16.6km climb, rising 1,190m, an average of 7.2 percent. There are two from the east, one from the Col de Soulor, a 1.247km climb over 30.1km (4.1 percent, but with a 6 percent gradient over the final 5.4km) or from the Cirque de Litor, rising 350m over 7.5km (4.6 percent gradient).

Characteristics: There are two narrow tunnels through which the riders go near to the summit and fearsome drops from the road. In 1951, Dutch rider Wim Van Est – the first Dutchman to wear the yellow jersey – slid off the road and fell 70m, surviving only because he landed on a tiny ledge. He was dragged to safety by rope.

Tour visits: 71 in total, but only two have finished at the summit.

Multiple winners:
4:	Federico Bahamontes	(1954, 1958, 1963, 1964)
3:	Ottavio Bottecchia	(1923, 1924, 1925)
2:	Lucien Buysse	(1926, 1929)
	Vicente Trueba	(1932, 1933)
	Jean Robic	(1947, 1950)
	Fausto Coppi	(1949, 1952)
	Julio Jiminez	(1965, 1968)

Conquerors of the peak: Stephen Roche (1985) and Michael Rasmussen (2007) were the winners on the only two occasions when a stage finished on the summit of the Col d'Aubisque.

Did You Know That?
The Col d'Aubisque was a feature of every Tour de France from 1910 to 1947.

❋ HINAULT SWEEPS UP ALL BEFORE HIM ❋

Bernard Hinault (Renault-Gitane) won a head-to-head final sprint on the Champs-Elysées against Joop Zoetemelk (Miko-Mercier) on the final stage of the 1979 Tour de France. Hinault, who was just 24 years old, also claimed his second successive Tour victory. Zoetemelk, however, failed the drug test (Nandrolone) on this final stage and was penalised 10 minutes. Amazingly, despite the 10-minute penalty Zoetemelk still finished second overall in the GC.

❋ THE BROOM WAGON ❋

When a mountain stage was first introduced to the Tour in 1910, Henri Desgrange added a "Broom Wagon" to follow the last rider and pick up any who were unable to finish. Desgrange stated that a rider unable to finish the stage in the Pyrenees could ride to the finish in the Broom Wagon and start the Tour again the next day.

❋ KING OF THE STAGES ❋

Eddy Merckx has won more stages of the Tour de France than any other rider in the history of the sport, with an amazing 34. In 1969 he won six stages plus the overall yellow jersey; eight in 1970 plus the overall yellow jersey; four in 1971 plus the overall yellow jersey; six in 1972 plus the overall yellow jersey; eight stages in 1974 plus the overall yellow jersey and two stages in 1975.

❋ TOUR SPOKESMEN (8) ❋

"It's the stuff of dreams … As a child, being a fan of the sport, I never imagined that one day I'd be in this position. Kids from Kilburn don't become favourite for the Tour de France. You're supposed to become a postman or a milkman or work in Ladbrokes."
Bradley Wiggins, British cyclist, winner of the 2012 Tour de France

❈ TOUR DE FRANCE WINNERS ❈

Year	Winner	Country
1903	Maurice Garin	France
1904	Henri Cornet	France
1905	Louis Trousselier	France
1906	René Pottier	France
1907	Lucien Petit-Brenton Mazan	France
1908	Lucien Petit-Brenton Mazan	France
1909	François Faber	Luxembourg
1910	Octave Lapize	France
1911	Gustave Garrigou	France
1912	Odile Defraye	Belgium
1913	Philippe Thys	Belgium
1914	Philippe Thys	Belgium
1919	Firmin Lambot	Belgium
1920	Philippe Thys	Belgium
1921	Léon Scieur	Belgium
1922	Firmin Lambot	Belgium
1923	Henri Pélissier	France
1924	Ottavio Bottecchia	Italy
1925	Ottavio Bottecchia	Italy
1926	Lucien Buysse	Belgium
1927	Nicolas Frantz	Luxembourg
1928	Nicolas Frantz	Luxembourg
1929	Maurice De Waele	Belgium
1930	André Leducq	France
1931	Antonin Magne	France
1932	André Leducq	France
1933	Georges Speicher	France
1934	Antonin Magne	France
1935	Romain Maes	Belgium
1936	Sylvére Maes	Belgium
1937	Roger Lapébie	France
1938	Gino Bartali	Italy
1939	Sylvére Maes	Belgium
1947	Jean Robic	France
1948	Gino Bartali	Italy
1949	Fausto Coppi	Italy
1950	Ferdi Kübler	Switzerland
1951	Hugo Koblet	Switzerland
1952	Fausto Coppi	Italy
1953	Louison Bobet	France

1954	Louison Bobet	France
1955	Louison Bobet	France
1956	Roger Walkowiak	France
1957	Jacques Anquetil	France
1958	Charly Gaul	Luxembourg
1959	Frederico Bahamontes	Spain
1960	Gastone Nencini	Italy
1961	Jacques Anquetil	France
1962	Jacques Anquetil	France
1963	Jacques Anquetil	France
1964	Jacques Anquetil	France
1965	Felice Gimondi	Italy
1966	Lucien Aimar	France
1967	Roger Pingeon	France
1968	Jan Janssen	Netherlands
1969	Eddy Merckx	Belgium
1970	Eddy Merckx	Belgium
1971	Eddy Merckx	Belgium
1972	Eddy Merckx	Belgium
1973	Luis Ocaña	Spain
1974	Eddy Merckx	Belgium
1975	Bernard Thévenet	France
1976	Lucien Van Impe	Belgium
1977	Bernard Thévenet	France
1978	Bernard Hinault	France
1979	Bernard Hinault	France
1980	Joop Zoetemelk	Netherlands
1981	Bernard Hinault	France
1982	Bernard Hinault	France
1983	Laurent Fignon	France
1984	Laurent Fignon	France
1985	Bernard Hinault	France
1986	Greg LeMond	USA
1987	Stephan Roche	Ireland
1988	Pedro Delgado	Spain
1989	Greg LeMond	USA
1990	Greg LeMond	USA
1991	Miguel Induráin	Spain
1992	Miguel Induráin	Spain
1993	Miguel Induráin	Spain
1994	Miguel Induráin	Spain
1995	Miguel Induráin	Spain
1996	Bjarne Riis	Denmark

1997	Jan Ullrich	Germany
1998	Marco Pantani	Italy
2006	Óscar Pereiro*	Spain
2007	Alberto Contador	Spain
2008	Carlos Sastre	Spain
2009	Alberto Contador	Spain
2010	Andy Schleck*	Luxembourg
2011	Cadel Evans	Australia
2012	Bradley Wiggins	Great Britain

* = Floyd Landis (2006) and Alberto Contador (2010) were stripped of wins. However, none of Lance Armstrong's seven Tour de France victories, 1999–2005 inclusive, were reassigned.

✳ KNIGHTS ON AND OFF THE ROAD ✳

Bradley Wiggins received a knighthood in the 2013 New Year Honours List, but so did his Team Sky coach, Dave Brailsford, who had been in charge of Team GB's cyclists at the London 2012 Olympic Games.

✳ SPEEDY TOUR ✳

The 1971 Tour covered 3,608 kilometres and was the shortest Tour since 1905. The 760km reduction in distance from the previous year resulted in the 1971 Tour setting a then record average speed of 37.29 kph, almost 2 kph faster than 1970.

✳ TOUR SPOKESMEN (9) ✳

"I've read that I flew up the hills and mountains of France. But you don't fly up a hill. You struggle slowly and painfully up a hill, and maybe, if you work very hard, you get to the top ahead of everybody else."
Lance Armstrong

✳ OPENING STAGE WIN TREBLE ✳

In the 1958 Tour de France, André Darrigade won the opening stage and the yellow jersey for the third successive year.

✳ TOUR SNUBS PARIS START ✳

For the first time since its inauguration in 1903, the 1926 Tour de France started somewhere other than Paris. It left instead from Evian, a small town in the Alps situated on Lake Geneva. The riders were transported to Evian on a chartered train.

✳ HINAULT CRASHES ✳

Bernard Hinault (La Vie Claire) crashed with a kilometre to go on Stage 14 of the 1985 Tour de France. After lying on the ground for several minutes he got back on his bike and crossed the line, his face a bloody mess from a broken nose.

✳ OVER THE RAINBOW ✳

On 3 October 2004, Oscar Freire (Spain) won the World Championships in Verona, Italy. It was Freire's third Rainbow Jersey (1999, 2001 and 2004), thereby joining an elite club of three times World Champions: Alfredo Binda (1927, 1930 and 1932), Rik Van Steenbergen (1949, 1956 and 1957) and Eddy Merckx (1967, 1971 and 1974).

✳ SPANISH TOUR WINNERS ✳

1	5 wins	Miguel Indurain (1991, 1992, 1993, 1994, 1995)
2	2 wins	Alberto Contador (2007, 2009)
3	1 win	Federico Bahamontes (1959)
=	1 win	Luis Ocaña (1973)
=	1 win	Pedro Delgado (1988)
=	1 win	Oscar Pereiro (2006)
=	1 win	Carlos Sastre (2008)

✳ ITALIAN WALKOUT ✳

Gino Bartali (Italy) won Stage 11 of the 1950 Tour de France, but he was so incensed with the way the French fans had kicked and punched him after he fell off his bike on the Aspin that he told his team boss Alfredo Binda that he was withdrawing from the race, and that the two Italian teams in the race should quit with him. Fiorenzo Magni (Italy) was having a spectacular Tour and was in the yellow jersey, 2 minutes 31 seconds ahead of Ferdy Kübler (Switzerland). Binda and Bartali stayed up most of the night at their hotel in St Gaudens debating the matter. The Tour boss, Jacques Goddet, suggested a number of compromises, including allowing the Italian riders to wear neutral grey jerseys to hide them from the crowds. However, while several of his team members wavered, Bartali remained adamant. As a result the Italians withdrew from the race before the start of Stage 12 and a later stage of the Tour that had been scheduled to end in the Italian town of San Remo was consequently cancelled.

THE TOUR'S FIRST GIRO WINNER

Luigi Ganna (Italy) lay in second place with 20 points to Lucien Petit-Breton (5 points) in the overall GC after Stage 3 of the 1908 Tour de France, his highest ever placing in the race. Prior to the 1908 Tour, Ganna had won the inaugural Giro d'Italia held the same year.

A DAY OF TRAGEDY

Stage 7 of the 1935 Tour de France took the riders over the Alps, going from Aix-les-Bains to Grenoble and facing climbs over the Télégraphe, the Galibier and the Lautaret. Antonin Magne, winner of the Tour in 1931 and 1934, was hit by a car on the Télégraphe and, badly injured, was taken to hospital in a farmer's cart. As a result of his injuries, Magne had to abandon the race. But then the first true tragedy in the history of the Tour de France struck: Francisco Cepeda, riding in the Tour as a Spanish *individuel*, crashed on the descent of the Galibier and fractured his skull. He died three days later to become the Tour's first fatality.

AN ENTERTAINING START

Josephine Baker, the American expatriate entertainer, started the 80 riders of the 1933 Tour de France.

NATIONAL TEAMS REINTRODUCED

As a result of the riders' strike during Stage 9 of the 1966 Tour de France the Tour organisers reverted to national teams for the 1967 and 1968 Tours. They believed that the sponsors were behind the strike and took steps to remove their influence.

THE INAUGURAL TOUR DE FRANCE

On 19 January 1903, just a few days after *L'Auto-Vélo* lost a lawsuit brought by *Le Vélo*, *L'Auto* (it had to change its name from *L'Auto-Vélo* as part of the lawsuit) announced the first Tour de France. *L'Auto* advertised it as "the greatest cycling trial in the entire world. A race more than a month long: Paris to Lyon to Marseille to Toulouse to Bordeaux to Nantes to Paris." The inaugural Tour de France was to be a race lasting five weeks starting on 31 May and ending on 5 July. *L'Auto* stipulated that the winner would be the rider with the lowest elapsed time after racing six stages.

❋ GREAT TOURS DE FRANCE (3): 1919 ❋

It had been only nine months since the First World War had ended and riders were faced with the longest-ever Tour to date (only the 1926 Tour would be longer) at 5,560km (3,455 miles), with each stage averaging 370km (230 miles) in length. Stage 5, from Les Sables-d'Olonne to Bayonne, covered 482km (300 miles), and was the longest stage ever. *L'Auto* newspaper was published on yellow paper and the Tour organisers decided that the race leader would be clearly identifiable if he wore yellow and, thus, the yellow jersey was born. The first man to wear it was Eugène Christophe, who had been the leader at the end of Stage 10. However, he was caught by Firmin Lambot on the penultimate stage and it was the Belgian who rode into Paris in yellow.

Rank	Name	Country	Time
1.	Firmin Lambot	Belgium	231h 07' 15"
2.	Jean Alavoine	France	+1h 42' 54"
3.	Eugène Christophe	France	+2h 26' 31"
4.	Léon Scieur	Belgium	+2h 52' 15"
5.	Honoré Barthélemy	France	+4h 14' 22"
6.	Jacques Coomans	Belgium	+15h 21' 34"
7.	Luigi Lucotti	Italy	+16h 01' 12"
8.	Joseph Van Daele	Belgium	+18h 23' 02"
9.	Alfred Steux	Belgium	+20h 29' 01"
10.	Jules Nempon	France	+21h 44' 12"

Did You Know That?
Two weeks after the end of the Tour, Paul Duboc, eighth overall, was disqualified after organisers found out he had borrowed a car to go to repair a broken axle on his bike. The final classification thus contained only 10 riders out of the 67 who started.

❋ TOUR SPOKESMEN (10) ❋

"Here's the routine I'd advise for the evening before a race: a pheasant with chestnuts, a bottle of champagne and a woman."
Jacques Anquetil, five-time Tour de France winner

❋ SWEDISH JOY ❋

Magnus Backstedt (GAN) won Stage 19 of the 1998 Tour de France to become the first Swedish rider to win a stage in the world's greatest cycle race.

❋ CAUGHT OUT SPEEDING ❋

Stage 12 of the 1971 Tour de France from Orcières-Merlette in the Alps to Marseilles had been ridden at such an intense speed that when Luciano Armani reached the finish line in Marseilles over two hours earlier than expected, there was no one there to greet him. Not surprisingly it was the fastest stage to date in Tour history, at 45.351 kilometres per hour.

❋ LUXEMBOURG'S SECOND ❋

In 1927, Nicolas Frantz (Alcyon) became the second Luxemburger – François Faber (1909) being the first – to win the Tour de France.

❋ HINAULT QUITS BEFORE THE START ❋

During the spring of 1983 Bernard Hinault won the Vuelta and the Flèche Wallonne, but during the Vuelta the tendonitis in his right knee flared up again. It was this same injury that had caused him to abandon the Tour in 1980 after Stage 12 and on the eve of the start of the 1983 Tour, Hinault announced that he would not be attempting to win a record five *maillots jaunes*. Laurent Fignon won the first of his two consecutive Tour victories in 1983.

❋ LE GRAND TOUR ❋

For the 1928 Tour de France Henri Desgrange tinkered with both the rules and the format of the race yet again. In addition to trade teams of sponsored professional riders and the independent *touriste-routiers*, he added nine French teams of *touriste-routiers* representing different regions of France, such as Alsace-Lorraine and Normandy. The peloton comprised 162 riders, a record at the time.

❋ PANTANI CLAIMS HIS FIRST YELLOW ❋

Marco Pantani, known as *"Il Pirata"* (the Pirate), won Stage 15 (189km with four major climbs in the ascent from Grenoble to Les Deux Alpes) of the 1998 Tour de France after a brilliant solo ride through the Alps finishing 8 minutes 59 seconds ahead of the defending champion, Germany's Jan Ullrich. The stage win meant that the Italian wore the *maillot jaune* for the first time in his career. He was the seventh different rider to don the leader's jersey in the 1998 Tour.

❋ NATIONAL TEAMS ABANDONED ❋

In 1929 the Tour de France's founder, Henri Desgrange, believed that the trade teams had colluded to fix the result of that year's Tour. Consequently in 1930 he banned trade teams in favour of the national team format. This format proved to be very successful for the next three decades; however in 1962 the organisers of the Tour de France abandoned the national team format and went back to trade teams. This was a direct result of pressure from the bicycle manufacturers, who argued that the industry's future was at stake. Jacques Anquetil, riding for the St Raphaël-Halyett team, won his second successive *maillot jaune*, his third overall.

❋ TOUR DEATHS (1) ❋

In 1910, Adolphe Hélière (France) drowned on the French Riviera during a Tour rest day.

❋ A CONSISTENT FINISHER ❋

In 1973 Luis Ocaña (Bic) won six stages on his way to winning the Tour de France. The Spanish rider finished in 122 hours 25 minutes 34 seconds with Bernard Thévenet (Peugeot) in second place at 15 minutes 51 seconds. In addition to claiming his *maillot jaune* Ocaña finished third in the climbers' competition to his fellow countryman Pedro Torres and third in the overall points competition to Herman Van Springel.

❋ GREEN WITH ENVY ❋

Fritz Schaer (Switzerland) was the inaugural winner of the overall green jersey in the 1953 Tour de France.

❋ FRENCH FORCE ❋

The French line-up that took part in the 1932 Tour de France was the finest they had entered since the race began in 1903. André Leducq, the 1930 winner, was joined by Georges Speicher (he would win the Tour in 1933), Roger Lapébie (winner in 1937), Marcel Bidot, Maurice Archambaud, Albert Barthélemy, Louis Péglion, and Julien Moineau. Meanwhile the Italians could count on three Giro d'Italia winners in their team: Luigi Marchisio, (1930), Francesco Camusso (1931) and Antonio Pesenti (1932).

❋ TOUR LEGENDS (3) – JACQUES ANQUETIL ❋

Jacques Anquetil was born on 8 January 1934 in Mont-Saint-Aigan, near Rouen, France. He began his racing career in 1951 and the following year he won the French amateur road title. In 1953, his first year as an independent (semi-professional) rider, he won the Grand Prix des Nations individual time trial and went on to win the race for the first of a record nine times. Three years later, Jacques broke Fausto Coppi's 14-year-old World Hour Record with a speed of 46.159 kph.

In 1957, at his first attempt, Anquetil won the Tour de France. After abandoning in 1958, Jacques finished third in 1959 and didn't enter in 1960, having won the Giro d'Italia earlier in the year. Prior to the 1961 Tour, Anquetil openly stated that he would claim the yellow jersey on the first day and wear it all the way to Paris, and he delivered on his bold promise. Anquetil was outstanding in time trials (as well as "Maître Jacques", "Monsieur Chrono" was another of his nicknames), and having won the part of Stage 1 to take the *maillot jaune*, he held off all-comers, eventually finishing more than 12 minutes clear of the field.

Having acquired the taste for the yellow jersey, Jacques feasted on it, becoming the first rider to win the Tour de France four successive times (1961–64), and the first five-time winner. None of his last three Tour victories was as dominant, and his final success was by only 55 seconds. The man who missed out in all three years (third in 1962, second in 1963 and 1964), was Raymond Poulidor, the greatest rider never to win the Tour.

Anquetil also enjoyed much success in the two other grand tours – the Giro d'Italia and Vuelta a España. He emulated Coppi by completing the Giro–Tour double in 1964 (he also enjoyed a pair of second- and third-place finishes in the Italian event), this a year after becoming the first man to achieve the Vuelta–Tour double.

A consummate road racer, he won 200 events in his career, including the Liège–Bastogne–Liège race in 1966, and the Paris–Nice competition five times. The one big regret for Anquetil's fans was that he never managed to win the World Championships and don the famous rainbow jersey – runner-up in 1966 was his best finish among six top 10s. When he retired from riding, he became a farmer like his father, an occasional race director for the Tour and a radio commentator.

He died in his sleep on 18 November 1987.

Did You Know That?
Jacques Anquetil was the first rider to win all three Grand Tours.

✻ THE GIANT TURNIP ✻

Stage 18 of the 1959 Tour de France took the riders on a 243-kilometre journey from Le Lauteret to St Vincent d'Aosta in Italy. During the stage, which was raced on a very hot day, the riders had to climb the Galibier (after 7 kilometres); the Iseran (after 114 kilometres); and the Petit Saint-Bernard (after 186 kilometres). Louison Bobet, the three-times Tour winner, abandoned the race when he reached the top of the Iseran, while Ercole Baldini took the stage victory. Spain's Federico Bahamontes was now in the leader's jersey, which he retained all the way to Paris, with France's Henry Anglade at 4 minutes 4 seconds. The great Tour de France writer Pierre Chany described this stage as a "giant turnip".

✻ TOUR SPOKESMEN (11) ✻

"You have no idea what the Tour de France is. It's a Calvary. Worse than that, because the road to the Cross has only 14 stations and ours has 15. We suffer from the start to the end."
Henri Pélissier, Tour de France winner

✻ INJURY RULES OUT FORMER WINNER ✻

Luis Ocaña, winner of the Tour de France in 1973, was forced to abandon the 1975 Tour with a knee problem on Stage 13 in the Massif Central.

✻ ITALY BACK IN YELLOW ✻

Stage 2 of the 1965 Tour de France took the riders from across the border from Liège in Belgium to Roubaix, France. Felice Gimondi, taking part in his first Tour, won the stage to claim his first-ever win as a professional and with it the yellow jersey. He was the first Italian to wear the leader's yellow jersey since Gastone Nencini won the Tour de France in 1960.

✻ EARLY COLOURS ✻

The famous yellow jersey was not presented to the Tour leader until 1919 but Maurice Garin, after winning the first-ever stage in the inaugural Tour de France in 1903, was given a green armband to signify that he was first in the general classification, while the rider in last position was given the "Lanterne Rouge" (Red Lantern).

✻ THE TOUR DE DOPAGE ✻

The 1998 Tour de France was dubbed the "Tour de Dopage" (the Dope Tour) as a direct result of the numerous doping scandals throughout the race. Before the Tour began, Willy Voet, a *soigneur* in the French Festina team, was arrested on his way into France and found to have large quantities of doping products in his team car. Following Voet's arrest a police raid found drugs in the rooms of the TVM team, resulting in the riders staging a sit-down protest at what they regarded as harsh treatment by the authorities. The Spanish teams pulled out of the 1998 Tour race when urged to do so by the ONCE team, led by the French national champion, Laurent Jalabert.

✻ AMERICAN TOUR WINNERS ✻

1 7 wins............Lance Armstrong* (1999, 2000, 2001, 2002,
2003, 2004, 2005)
2 3 wins................................Greg LeMond (1986, 1989, 1990)
3 1 win...Floyd Landis* (2006)

* Lance Armstrong and Floyd Landis were both stripped of their respective Tour titles by the cycling authorities for drugs offences. Landis's victory was given to Oscar Perreiro (Spain), but the seven Tours 1999–2005 have been left unassigned.

✻ FIRST BRITISH STAGE VICTORY ✻

Brian Robinson made Tour de France history in Stage 7 of the 1958 race by becoming the first British rider to win a stage. In a chase to the line Robinson sprinted against the Italian rider, Arrigo Padovan, and although Padovan crossed the finish line first, he was subsequently relegated to second place by the race officials for what they termed "irregular sprinting". Robinson was a member of a multi-national team named "Internations" which included other British riders, an Irish rider (Seamus Elliot) and riders from Austria, Denmark and Portugal.

✻ TOUR SPOKESMEN (12) ✻

"A rider says to me, 'I go out training two hours every morning.' But I ask him, 'What about the afternoon?'"
Sean Kelly, multiple winner of the green jersey in the Tour de France

❋ THYS THE MAN ❋

Henri Desgrange had slated Philippe Thys in the pages of *L'Auto* over the Belgian rider's poor performance in the 1919 Tour de France, but the truth was that Thys should not have ridden in the 1919 Tour at all since he was in no fit shape to ride and was in fact unable to finish the first stage. However, with the harsh words of Desgrange driving him on, Thys resumed his regime of hard work and trained assiduously over the winter of 1919. By the start of the 1920 season Thys was ready to take on anyone and everyone, although things didn't look good when he broke his collarbone in a crash in Milan–San Remo in March 1920. The gritty Belgian nevertheless finished the remaining 50 kilometres of that race and by the time the 1920 Tour de France came round he was ready. Thys rode for the manufacturer's consortium La Sportive, who were managed by Alphonse Baugé, architect of many of both Peugeot's and Alcyon's pre-war Tour de France victories. Thys won the 1920 Tour, his third after winning the yellow jersey in 1913 and 1914.

❋ SPECTATOR PUNCHES MERCKX ❋

Stage 14 of the 1975 Tour de France, culminating in a finish at the top of Puy de Dôme, was a defining moment that altered the course of that year's race. Four kilometres from the stage finish, Lucien van Impe and Bernard Thévenet dropped Eddy Merckx, the yellow jersey leader. Then just a few hundred metres from the finish, a spectator jumped out of the crowd and punched Merckx in the stomach. Van Impe won the stage by 15 seconds over Thévenet, while Merckx continued on and finished at 49 seconds behind the stage winner. When he crossed the line Merckx threw up and then rode back down the climb to identify his attacker, who claimed it was an accident. Merckx retained his yellow jersey by 58 seconds but had to take painkillers and blood thinners to relieve his discomfort. In Stage 15 Merckx found his energy had deserted him, which eventually led to him losing his yellow jersey and his chances of rewriting history by claiming a record sixth Tour win.

❋ THE FIRST-EVER PELOTON ❋

At precisely 3.16pm on 1 July 1903, a peloton of 60 riders departed from Café au Réveil-Matin in Montgeron, situated in the southern outskirts of Paris, on the inaugural stage of the first-ever Tour de France.

❋ GREAT CLIMBS (3) – COL D'IZOARD ❋

Just six of the 92 Alpine climbs in the history of the Tour de France have gone higher than the 2,361m of the Col d'Izoard, and of those half-dozen, only the Galibier (at 2,645m) has been visited more than a handful of times. Izoard is a bleak, energy-sapping climb, frequently starting, finishing or going through Briançon, the highest town (with a population of at least 2,000) in the European Union. At the top of the Izoard is a small cycling museum and memorial to Louison Bobet, the only three-time stage winner, and the great Italian Fausto Coppi who won twice here.

Location: The département of Haut-Alpes and region of Provence-Alpes-Côtes d'Azur, close to France's border with Italy.

Nearest town: Briançon.

Height: The stage finish is at 2,361m.

Gradient: The climb north from Guillestre is 15.9km, with an average gradient of 6.9 percent. From Briançon to the Col it is 20km and an average gradient of 5.8 percent.

Characteristics: Known as the *Cassé Desert* (broken desert), the road is barren and forbidding with scree slopes and protruding pillars of weathered rock, especially on the upper south side.

Tour visits: 30.

Multiple winners: 3: Louison Bobet (1950, 1953, 1954)
2: Nicolas Frantz (1924, 1927), Sylvère Maes (1936, 1939), Gino Bartali (1938, 1948), Fausto Coppi (1949, 1951).

Conquerors of the peak: Philippe Thys (1922), Henri Pélissier (1923), Julien Berrendero (1937), Jean Robic (1947), Valentin Huot (1956), Federico Bahamontes (1958), Imerio Massignan (1960), Joaquim Galera (1965), Eddy Merckx (1972), José-Manuel Fuente (1973), Bernard Thévenet (1975), Lucien Van Impe (1976), Eduardo Chozas (1986), Pascal Richard (1989), Claudio Chiappucci (1993), Santiago Botero (2000), Aitor Garmendia (2003), Stefano Garzelli (2006), Maxim Iglinsky (2011).

Did You Know That?
In the 15 Tours de France since Louison Bobet completed his hat-trick of stage wins on the Izoard in 1956, no rider has won a stage there more than once.

❋ POINTS SYSTEM INTRODUCED ❋

The winner of the first two Tour de France races was declared according to the time taken, but from 1905 it would be decided on points. Henri Desgrange believed that the introduction of a points scoring system would help reduce cheating. A rider was awarded a point for winning a stage, two points for coming second and so on, so that the rider with the fewest points, when all his stage placings were added up, won the Tour. Consequently if a rider managed to win all 11 stages of the Tour in 1905 he would have amassed 11 points. This method of determining the winner of the yellow jersey was used up until 1913. The 1905 Tour also witnessed the introduction of mountain stages for the first time, when the riders raced through the Vosges Mountains in eastern France with the Ballon d'Alsace and the Col Bayard climbs. Louis Trousselier (France) won the Tour that year with 35 points.

❋ HARD AS NAILS ❋

In Stage 9 of the 1920 Tour de France, Honoré Barthélémy suffered a serious crash. His back was so badly hurt he had to twist his handlebars upwards so that he wouldn't have to bend over too far. A road chipping had also pierced one of his eyes, resulting in a permanent loss of vision. Bruised, half blind and bleeding heavily, he removed the flint from his eye, remounted his bike and finished the stage. Barthélémy crashed several more times after Stage 9; as well as losing the sight in one eye and ruining his back, he suffered a broken wrist and a dislocated shoulder in subsequent falls.

❋ THE SORCERER AND HIS APPRENTICE ❋

When Henri Pélissier (Automoto) won the 1923 Tour de France he became the first French victor since Gustave Garrigou in 1911. Pélissier spoke very highly of his teammate Ottavio Bottecchia, the young Italian rider who was making his Tour debut, stating: "Bottecchia will succeed me." Bottecchia won the 1924 and 1925 Tours, becoming the first Italian to win the race.

✳ ALL CHANGE IN THE TOUR ✳

In 1965 Emilion Amaury, the publisher and Second World War resistance fighter who had influenced the French Cycling Federation's decision to award the Tour to Jacques Goddet after the war, purchased Goddet's *L'Equipe* sports newspaper and the Tour de France itself. Despite winning the four previous Tours de France, Jacques Anquetil decided not to ride in the 1965 Tour, believing he could earn more money by concentrating on winning the post-Tour Critérium races. There is no doubt that had Anquetil ridden in the 1965 Tour, he would have claimed his fifth consecutive *maillot jaune* because he was in majestic form winning the Dauphiné Libéré, and then that afternoon flew to the midnight start of Bordeaux–Paris, which he also won. He crossed the finish line first in Paris–Nice and the Critérium National, and was third in the French National Championships.

✳ TOUR SPOKESMEN (13) ✳

"If the average person could try cycling, he'd say, 'My God, I can't believe how tough it is.' Everybody says how tough a marathon is, but 25,000 people show up to start a marathon in New York. Only 200 people can start the Tour de France."
Greg LeMond, former pro cyclist and Tour de France winner

✳ SPAIN'S FIRST *MAILLOT JAUNE* ✳

The 1955 Tour de France started in northern France and headed east towards Belgium with a split stage on the first day of racing. In the morning the riders rode 102 kilometres from Le Havre to Dieppe, and the Spanish rider Miguel Poblet entered the Tour's history books when he won the stage and became the first Spanish rider to wear the *maillot jaune*. The Dutch team won the afternoon's 12.5km team time trial and Poblet retained the yellow jersey.

✳ THE *MAILLOT JAUNE* ✳

During the 1919 Tour de France Henri Desgrange unveiled the yellow jersey (*maillot jaune*) for the first time. The jersey signified the leader of the Tour and Firmin Lambot (Belgium) became the first rider to wear it. Lambot, a two-times winner of the Tour (1919 and 1922), worked as a saddler before he began racing professionally in 1908.

PARLIAMENT SUSPENDED

Stage 20 of the 1987 Tour de France, a tough Alpine route that included the First Category Cote de Laffrey and ended with the *Hors Catégorie* l'Alpe d'Huez, left its mark on Spanish politics. Federico Echave won the stage, but the real race was between Spain's Pedro Delgado and Ireland's Stephen Roche. Roche was in yellow but the Spaniard finished in front of him with enough of a margin over the *maillot jaune*, 25 seconds, to claim the jersey for himself. Spain was so immersed in the Tour and the excitement of Delgado's battle with Roche for the yellow jersey that the Spanish parliament suspended proceedings so that members could watch it on TV.

THE TOUR JOINS UCI PROTOUR

Since 2005, the Tour de France has been a part of the UCI ProTour series of bike races. The ProTour includes the three Grand Tours, namely the Tour de France, Giro d'Italia and Vuelta a España. The ProTour also comprises most of the former UCI World Cup races, including Paris–Roubais, Tour of Flanders and Liège–Bastogne–Liège.

STARS AND STRIPES TOUR

In 1986, the first-ever American team entered the Tour de France. "7 Eleven-Hoonved" entered the race with Bob Roll, Alexi Grewal (the 1984 Olympic gold medallist), Chris Carmichael, Eric Heiden, Alex Stieda, Jeff Pierce, Raul Alcala, Davis Phinney, Doug Shapiro (who had ridden on Joop Zoetemelk's Kwantum-Decosol team in 1985) and Ron Kiefel.

THE MOUNTAINEER

Octave Lapize (France) was the first rider to reach the top of a mountain climb when he went over the Peyresourde, the first of four climbs in the Pyrenees, on Stage 5 of the 1910 Tour de France. By winning the stage he also became the first rider to claim victory in the mountains, and he went on to win the yellow jersey. Before that year's Tour, Lapize had already won Paris–Roubaix twice as well as finishing second in Paris–Brussels. Lapize went on to win a third Paris–Roubaix as well as three Paris–Brussels and three Championships of France, but he never again finished the Tour despite four more attempts.

❉ GREAT TOURS DE FRANCE (4): 1949 ❉

The era just before and just after the Second World War was dominated by Italian cyclists and maybe the country's two greatest, Gino Bartali and Fausto Coppi, went head-to-head in 1949. Coppi was named as Italy's lead rider, a move which almost led to Bartali withdrawing before the Tour; once it was under way, however, Coppi felt that his compatriot was not giving him the support a team leader deserved and threatened to abandon. France's Jacques Marinelli led for six stages before a third Italian, Fiorenzo Magni, took over, until Stage 15. The first Alpine stage was won by Bartali, but Coppi relieved him of the yellow jersey after the next mountain stage. A superb time trial in the penultimate stage ensured Coppi finished almost 11 minutes clear of the field, Marinelli 25 minutes adrift in third place.

Rank	Name	Country	Time
1.	Fausto Coppi	Italy	149h 40' 49"
2.	Gino Bartali	Italy	+10' 55"
3.	Jacques Marinelli	France	+25' 13"
4.	Jean Robic	France	+34' 28"
5.	Marcel Dupont	Belgium	+38' 59"
6.	Fiorenzo Magni	Italy	+42' 10"
7.	Stan Ockers	Belgium	+44' 35"
8.	Jean Goldschmit	Luxembourg	+47' 24"
9.	Apo Lazaridès	France	+52' 28"
10.	Pierre Cogan	France	+1h 08' 55"

Did You Know That?
Mountain categories only began in 1948, when there were two; a year later, a third category was added. Today there is *hors catégorie* for the highest mountains and four other categories of climb.

❉ THE TOUR ENTERS THE MOUNTAINS ❉

The introduction of a mountain stage in the Pyrenees in 1910, which involved climbing the Peyresourde, the Aspin, the Tourmalet and the Aubisque, was such a success that in 1911 an Alps stage was added, namely the massive Col du Galibier. The fifth stage of the 1911 Tour de France covered 366 kilometres from Chamonix to Grenoble, crossing the Aravis, the Télégraphe and the Col du Galibier. Emile Georget won the stage, a remarkable feat given that he had crashed two days earlier coming down the Ballon d'Alsace while attempting to avoid a motorcycle going in the opposite direction.

❋ TOUR SPOKESMEN (14) ❋

"He climbs like artists paint water colours, without any apparent extra effort. It's a mystery because when all is said and done Coppi has only two legs, two lungs, one heart, just like all the other Tour contestants."
André Leducq, about Fausto Coppi

❋ THE TOUR GOES INTERNATIONAL ❋

In 1907 the Tour went international for the first time when the route went via Germany. Henri Desgrange requested and received permission from the German government for the 1907 Tour de France to go to Metz in Alsace-Lorraine, territory ceded by France following the Franco-Prussian war.

❋ MERCKX'S MOST BEAUTIFUL TOUR ❋

Eddy Merckx (Faema) won the 1969 Tour de France, his first, by the widest margin of victory (17 minutes 54 seconds) since Fausto Coppi's 28-minute lead over Stan Ockers in 1952. Merckx also won all the other Tour competition jerseys including the "Combine" classification, points competition, and King of the Mountains. And to top things off, Merckx's team, Faema, won the Team General Classification. Some years later in an interview in *L'Equipe*, Merckx said, "I'd love to ride the 1969 Tour again, my first. I'd ride it the same way. It is my most beautiful memory, by a long way."

❋ AUSSIE COMES CLOSE ❋

To help prepare for the 1928 Tour de France Hubert Opperman, the three-times Australian cycling champion who was entering his maiden Tour, took part in several French road races and even managed to finish in third place in the Paris–Brussels race behind Nicolas Frantz (the 1928 Tour winner) and George Ronsse.

❋ WELCOME HOME ❋

During the 1969 Tour de France Stage 1b, a 15.6-kilometre team time trial in the Belgian city of Wolowe-St Pierre passed by the front door of Eddy Merckx's parents' grocery store. The home favourite did not disappoint as his Faema squad won the stage while Merckx also took control of the yellow jersey.

✹ FIVE ON THE TROT ✹

During the 1909 Tour de France, Luxembourg's François Faber won five consecutive stages for the Alcyon team (Stages 2–6). This incredible feat remains unequalled today and is highly unlikely ever to be matched. In Stage 4, as Faber came into Lyon, his chain broke but the Giant of Colombes casually got off his bike and ran at full speed, pushing his bike along the wet streets. Then in Stage 5, the wind on the Col de Porte was so strong that it twice knocked Faber off his bike. And incredibly, also during Stage 5, a horse knocked him off his bike and kicked his bike away. However, an undeterred Faber remounted a third time and pressed on to victory.

✹ FRANCE'S SOLO VICTORY ✹

Pascal Lino's Stage 14 win of the 1993 Tour de France was the only stage victory in the Tour that year by a French rider.

✹ ITALIAN TOUR WINNERS ✹

1	2 wins	Ottavio Bottecchia (1924, 1925)
=	2 wins	Gino Bartali (1938, 1948)
=	2 wins	Fausto Coppi (1949, 1952)
4	1 win	Gastone Nencini (1960)
=	1 win	Felice Gimondi (1965)
=	1 win	Marco Pantani (1998)

✹ CAEN YOU FINISH? ✹

Stage 22 of the 1933 Tour de France was scheduled to finish in the Caen Velodrome, but when too many riders arrived at the velodrome simultaneously, race officials decided to hold a one-lap time trial for first place. Amazingly René Le Grevès, who was two hours behind the yellow jersey of Georges Speicher, won the stage. However it was Speicher who stood atop the podium in Paris at the end of Stage 23 to claim his sole Tour de France overall victory.

✹ JOURNALISTS FALL TO THEIR DEATH ✹

On 14 July 1957, motorcycle rider Rene Wagter and his passenger Alex Virot, a journalist for Radio Luxembourg, both died when their bike slipped on gravel which forced them off a road without any support railing in the mountains near Ax-les-Thermes.

✱ THE LONGEST DAY ✱

Stage 5 of the 1924 Tour de France, from Les Sables d'Olonne to Bayonne, has the distinction of being the longest day by time in the Tour's history. Desgrange had first introduced this 482-kilometre stage in 1919 and it is considered to be the longest in distance of any Tour stage. In 1924, the stage winner took an exhausting 19 hours 40 minutes to complete the distance. The stage was never used again in the Tour.

✱ A BRIGHT STAR ✱

At the start of the 1907 season Lucien Petit-Breton, winner of the Tour the same year, won the first Milan–San Remo.

✱ CHAMPS-ELYSEES WELCOMES THE TOUR ✱

In 1975, for the first time in the Tour's 73-year history, the race ended on the Champs-Elysées, thereby ending the Tour's long history of finishing at velodromes. Between 1903 and 1967 the Tour ended at the Parc des Princes, while from 1968 to 1974 it ended at the Municipal Velodrome, commonly referred to as the "Cipale". Bernard Thévenet was the first rider to claim overall victory on the Champs-Elysées, and Eddy Merckx was the last rider to win the overall yellow jersey in a velodrome.

✱ CHUCKED OUT FOR HOLDING ON ✱

Stage 8 of the 1938 Tour de France was a classic Pyrenean stage, from Pau to Luchon with the usual quartet of monster climbs en route: the Aubisque, the Tourmalet, the Aspin and the Peyresourde. Georges Speicher (France), the 1933 Tour winner, was thrown out of the race for holding on to a car on the climbs. No doubt the judges did not wish to face a recurrence of the previous year's débâcle, which saw the Belgian team pack their bags when Roger Lapébie was given a mere ticking off for the same infraction of the rules.

✱ YOU'RE FIRED ✱

A few days before the end of the 2006 Tour de France, which Jan Ullrich missed, the German rider and winner of the Tour in 1997 received a fax from his team, T-Mobile, informing him that his services were no longer required.

✵ TOUR SPOKESMEN (15) ✵

"From snowstorm, water, ice, Batali rose majestically like an angel covered in mud, wearing under his soaked tunic the precious soul of a champion. It took this day of apocalypse to show his quality."
Jacques Goddet, after a tough day's ride, 1948

✵ FIRST ITALIAN IN YELLOW ✵

In his debut Tour de France in 1923, Ottavio Bottecchia (Automoto) finished second in Stage 1 and then won Stage 2 from Le Havre to Cherbourg. His victory in Stage 2 placed him in the overall lead, making him the first Italian ever to wear the yellow jersey. However, he lost the leader's jersey in the Alps to the man who went on to claim overall victory in Paris, his teammate Henri Pélissier from France.

✵ RIDER REFUSES DRUGS ✵

In 1998, Britain's former world pursuit champion Graeme Obree claimed in an interview with the *Express* newspaper that he had been asked to hand over £2,000 for "medical back-up" when he considered riding in the 1995 Tour de France. Obree claimed that the offer came from an English-speaking cyclist who – in Obree's opinion – was offering drugs, mainly erythropoietin (EPO). On 17 July 1993 at the Hamar Velodrome in Norway, Obree broke the one-hour distance record, held for nine years by Francesco Moser, with a distance of 51.596 kilometres. However, the Scottish rider's record lasted less than a week before it was broken by Chris Boardman. On 27 April 1994 Obree retook the record and was also the Individual Pursuit World Champion in 1993 and 1995.

✵ MR STUBBORN ✵

Henri Pélissier's stubborn, angry side manifested itself yet again on Stage 5 of the 1920 Tour de France. Pélissier discarded a spent tyre and Henri Desgrange handed him a two-minute penalty because Tour rules stipulated that a rider must end a stage with everything he had at the start, including clothing and tyres. Pélissier defiantly quit the Tour while Desgrange made fun of him in the pages of *L'Auto*, stating that the French rider did not know how to suffer and that he would never win the Tour de France. In 1923 Pélissier forced Desgrange to eat his words, as he claimed the yellow jersey in Paris.

✱ BROKEN SHOULDER IN A YELLOW JERSEY ✱

On Stage 11 of the 1983 Tour de France Pascal Simon crashed and broke his shoulder while wearing the yellow jersey. However, the plucky rider remounted and with help from his team he somehow managed to finish the stage in 61st place. Simon continued racing in the Tour and held the *maillot jaune* for the following six stages before finally being forced to abandon the Tour on Stage 17. Laurent Fignon was the new race leader.

✱ FAT-BOTTOMED GIRLS ✱

In 1978, the Tour de France inspired the lead singer of Queen, Freddie Mercury, to write the song "Bicycle Race". The song was released as a double A-side along with "Fat-Bottomed Girls".

✱ STAGE SHORTENED ✱

Stage 9 of the 1996 Tour de France was scheduled to be a 190-kilometre ride from Val d'Isère to Sestriere but the appalling weather conditions, including a heavy snowfall, meant the Tour organisers cut the stage to just 46 kilometres. Bjarne Riis won the stage and opened a crucial 44-second gap over his Telekom teammate Jan Ullrich, who was taking part in his maiden Tour. Riis went on to win the 1996 Tour, while Ullrich finished second overall at 1m 41s.

✱ ROBBED OF GLORY ✱

Hector Heusghem (Thomann) of Belgium took over the yellow jersey of the 1922 Tour de France after Stage 12, and held a 3 minutes 13 seconds lead over Firmin Lambot (Peugeot) in second place in the GC. In Stage 13 Heusghem wrecked his bike on a pothole and borrowed a teammate's machine to finish the stage. In 1922 the rules stated that riders had to repair their own bikes, and bike-swapping was normally forbidden. Heusghem had sought and received permission from a race official to swap bikes, but after reviewing the rules the judges gave the Belgian a one-hour time penalty, edging him outside the top three places in the GC. It proved to be the difference between victory and fourth place for Heusghem because at the end of the 1922 Tour de France he finished fourth overall, at 43 minutes 56 seconds behind the winner, Lambot.

❋ TOUR LEGENDS (4) – EDDY MERCKX ❋

Eddy Merckx was born on 17 June 1945 in Meensel-Kiezegem, Vlaams Brabant, Belgium. He began his amateur career in 1961 and, within three years, was World Amateur Road Race Champion. In 1965 he turned professional and the following year claimed his first professional victory, Six Days of Gent (partnering Patrick Sercu in this pairs event). Eddy won the 1966 Milan–San Remo, two stages in the 1967 Giro d'Italia and was crowned World Professional Road Race Champion.

It was not until 1968 that Eddy commenced his total domination of the Grand Tours by winning the Giro d'Italia, the first Belgian to claim the famous pink jersey. Merckx made his Tour de France debut in 1969 and not only won the overall classification (the first Belgian to win the Tour since Sylvère Maes in 1939) and the yellow jersey, he took the King of the Mountains prize (polka dot jersey) and points championship or sprinters' prize (green jersey) into the bargain, the only man ever to complete the Trifecta in one Tour. Merckx became the second man to win the Tour on five occasions with further victories in 1970, 1971, 1972 and 1974, and he still holds the Tour records for the most stage wins (34) and the most days in the yellow jersey (96).

But it wasn't just the Grand Tours at which Merckx excelled. He was a voracious collector of trophies and his appetite for all types of road racing earned him the nickname of the "The Cannibal". One of only three riders to have won the Giro d'Italia five times (he also enjoyed 24 stage wins), Eddy also took the 1973 Vuelta a España (and he won six stages in his career). He also won his home Tour de Belgique twice, and the 1974 Tour of Switzerland. In the Classic races, Merckx won the Milan–San Remo seven times, Liège–Bastogne–Liège five times and the World Road Racing Championship a record three times; all three are records. Eddy claimed three victories in Paris–Roubaix, and he also won at least one of all the Classics, with the exception of Paris–Tours.

Eddy retired from racing in 1978 at the age of 33, and established his own bicycle factory. A station on the Brussels metro is named in his honour while the same station has his World Hour Speed Record bike on display. De Grote Prijs Eddy Merckx (The Eddy Merckx Grand Prix), a cycle race, is named in his honour.

Did You Know That?
Only Laurent Jalabert has come close to matching Merckx's achievement of winning the overall, mountains and points titles in one Grand Tour. Jalabert claimed all three jerseys in the 1995 Vuelta a España.

❋ THE FIRST *MAILLOT JAUNE* ❋

The official history of the Tour de France states that Eugène Christophe (France) was the first rider to wear the yellow jersey in the race when he was presented with it after Stage 10 in 1919. However, the 1913 Tour winner Philippe Thys (Belgium) claimed that Henri Desgrange asked him to wear a unique distinguishing jersey as the Tour's leader in that year. Thys further claimed that he had declined the offer, feeling that it would essentially paint a large target on his back for the other riders to see. Thys' Peugeot team however quickly recognised the marketing potential of having their rider identified as the leader of the Tour de France, and he relented and wore a yellow jersey after all.

❋ TOUR SPOKESMEN (16) ❋

"The ideal tour would be one in which only one rider survived the ordeal."
Henri Desgrange, *founder of the Tour de France*

❋ CHEATED OUT OF VICTORY ❋

There is no doubt in the minds of many commentators that Greg LeMond, and not his La Vie Claire teammate Bernard Hinault, should have won the 1985 Tour de France. On Stage 17, LeMond and Stephen Roche pulled away from the rest of the leaders on the final climb to Luz Ardiden, with Hinault struggling some minutes behind. Roger Legeay, the La Vie team assistant director, drove up next to LeMond and the young American rider asked for permission to attack Roche and take the stage win. Legeay passed on LeMond's request and LeMond was told to wait for Hinault since he was only 40 seconds behind. As LeMond waited and waited, other riders including Phil Anderson and Sean Kelly caught up with him, but there was still no sign of Hinault. At the end of the stage, won by Pedro Delgado, LeMond was furious with team director Paul Koechli, as he knew he could have won the stage and ultimately taken the yellow jersey away from Hinault who was chasing his fifth Tour de France victory. In an interview with Bryan Malessa in 1999, LeMond said the team had lied to him about how far behind him Hinault actually was. LeMond finished 2 minutes 52 seconds behind Delgado, while Hinault was 4 minutes 5 seconds behind the Spaniard. LeMond lost the 1985 Tour de France to Hinault by 1 minute 42 seconds.

❊ NICKNAMES ❊

Rider	Nickname
Djamolidine Abdoujaparov	The Tashkent Terror
Ugo Agostini	Poncia
Jean Alavoine	Gars Jean
Robert Alban	Ban-ban
Eleuterio Anguita	El Lute
Jacques Anquetil	Maître Jacques, Monsieur Chrono
Maurice Archambaud	Chubby Cheeks
Hippolyte Aucouturier	Le Terrible
Federico Bahamontes	The Eagle of Toledo
Gianbattista Baronchelli	Gibi
Gino Bartali	Il Pio (The Pious), Il Vecchio (The Old Man)
Jean-François Bernard	Jeff
Julián Berrendero	El Negro (The Dark One)
Michael Boogerd	Boogi
Bernard Borreau	Petit frère (Little Brother)
Ottavio Bottecchia	Le Maçon de Frioul (The Bricklayer of Frioul)
Francesco Casagrande	Casseta
Mark Cavendish	The Manx Missile
Claudio Chiappucci	Il Diablo (The Devil)
Franco Chioccioli	Coppino
Eugène Christophe	Cri-cri, Le Vieux Gallois (The Old Gaul)
Mario Cipollini	Super Mario
Thierry Claveyrolat	Clavette, The Eagle of Vizille
Salvatore Commesso	Toto
Fausto Coppi	Il Campionissimo, Il Airone (The Heron)
Henri Cornet	The Joker
André Darrigade	Dédé
Pedro Delgado	Perico
Laurent Dufaux	Duduf
Jacky Durand	Dudu
Viacheslav Ekimov	Slava, Yeki
Federico Extabe	El Potro (The Foal) de Kortezubi
François Faber	The Giant of Colombes
Laurent Fignon	Le Professeur
Maurice Garin	The Little Chimney-Sweep
Stefano Garzelli	Piratino (Little Pirate)
Charly Gaul	The Angel of the Mountains
Raphaël Géminiani	Le Grand Fusil (Top Gun), Gem
Ivan Gotti	Bimbo
Learco Guerra	The Human Locomotive

Andy Hampsten	Ernie
Jens Heppner	Heppe
Luis Herrera	Lucho, The Little Gardener
Bernard Hinault	Le Blaireau (The Badger)
George Hincapié	Big George, Captain Blueheart, Mr No Chain
Miguel Indurain	Big-Mig, El Rey (The King)
Laurent Jalabert	Jaja
Bobby Julich	Bobby J
Sean Kelly	King Kelly, Mr Paris–Nice
Marcel Kint	The Black Eagle
Gerrie Knetemann	Kneet
Hugo Koblet	Le Pédaleur du Charme
Ferdy Kübler	Pedalling Madman, The Eagle of Adilswil
Hennie Kuiper	The Gentleman
Octave Lapize	Le Frisé (Curly)
Luc Leblanc	Stuart
André Leducq	Le Joyeux Dédé
Greg LeMond	Le Monster
Sylvère Maes	Le Père Futé (The Crafty Father)
Antonin Magne	The Taciturn, The Monk, Tonin the Silent
Thierry Marie	Titi
Eddy Merckx	Le Cannibale
Francesco Moser	Cecco
Johan Museeuw	De Leeuw van Vlaanderen (The Lion of Flanders)
Gastone Nencini	Le Lion de Mugello
Stuart O'Grady	Stuey, Freckle
Marco Pantani	Diabolino (Little Devil), Elefantino, Nosferatu, The Pirate
Lucien Petit-Breton	The Argentine
Eddy Planckaert	Die Kleine (The Small One)
Lucien Pothier	The Butcher of Sens
René Pottier	The First King of the Mountains
Raymond Poulidor	Pou-pou, The Eternal Second
Bjarne Riis	The Eagle of Herning, Mr 60%
Jean Robic	Old Leatherhead
Toni Rominger	El Martillo (The Hammer), The Camel
Peter Sagan	The Terminator
Léon Scieur	The Locomotive
Tommy Simpson	Four-Stone Coppi, Mister Tom
Dietrich Thurau	Didi
Philippe Thys	Fat Dog
Vicente Trueba	The Flea of Torrelavega
Jan Ullrich	Der Junge Jan, The Kaiser

❋ CHAMP GOES WRONG WAY ❋

During Stage 11 of the 1955 Tour de France Ferdy Kübler, Tour winner in 1950, started to weave across the road on Mount Ventoux. He stopped in a café for a while, got something to drink, and then remounted. However, like Abdel Khader Zaaf before him during the 1950 Tour, Kübler took off in the wrong direction. He abandoned the race the following day. Another rider, Jean Malléjac, was also suffering on the road up to the summit of Mount Ventoux. Just 10 kilometres from the top he began to swerve and weave across the road before falling to the ground. With one foot still strapped into the pedal, he tried to turn the crank as he lay on the road. Pierre Dumas, the Tour doctor, had to prise Malléjac's mouth open to administer medicine before he was taken to hospital in an ambulance, his Tour over.

❋ JACQUES IN THE YELLOW ❋

Jacques Anquetil won his first Tour de France yellow jersey during the 1957 race when he was among a small group of riders who managed to finish Stage 5, from Roubaix to Charleroi, two minutes ahead of the nearest chasers. Anquetil took the yellow jersey in his inaugural Tour de France by 1 minute 1 second from Marcel Janssens, and went on to claim overall victory in Paris.

❋ TOUR SPOKESMEN (17) ❋

"In Bobet's eyes, there were no little races or unimportant victories. Every race mattered and he wanted to give his all to his public. Bobet knew only one way to race, whatever the sacrifices."
Jacques Anquetil, on Louison Bobet

56

🌸 GREAT CLIMBS (4) – COL DE LA CROIX-DE-FER 🌸

As would be expected, Tour de France riders climbing the Col de la Croix-de-Fer, in the high Alps, pass an iron cross on the way to the 2,067m summit. The Col has been visited 16 times on the Tour, but it has never been either the start or the finish of a stage. The Col de la Croix-de-Fer does not receive as much publicity as most climbs in excess of 2,000m, mainly because almost every Tour de France stage passing this Col also visits the Col de Galibier, one of the four most legendary mountains of the Tour.

Location: The département of Savoie and region of Rhône-Alpes in eastern France.

Nearest town: Saint-Sorlin-d'Arves.

Height: 2,067m.

Gradient: From Saint Jean de Maurienne, riders climb 1522m over 30k, an average gradient of 5.1 percent, but it is 8.2 percent over the last 6km.

Characteristics: A particularly difficult climb, especially from the east/south-east, the road (the D926) zigzags up the Col, passing a small lake, Le Laitelet, a half-kilometre from the summit.

Tour visits: 16.

Multiple winners: None.

Conquerors of the peak: Fermo Camellini (1947), Gino Bartali (1948), Fausto Coppi (1952), René Marigil (1956), Guy Ignolin (1961), Claude Mattio (1963), Joaquim Galera (1966), Bernard Hinault (1986), Gert-Jan Theunise (1989), Eric Boyer (1992), Richard Virenque (1995), Rodolfo Massi (1998), Stéphane Heulot (1999), Michael Rasmussen (2006), Peter Velits (2008), Fredrik Kessiakof (2012).

🌸 A LONG WAIT 🌸

Gino Bartelli (Italy) holds the record for the longest period of time between overall Tour de France victories, winning his first Tour in 1938 and his last in 1948.

❋ A HOT STAGE ❋

Stage 12 of the 1986 Tour de France took the race into the Pyrenees, with three highly rated climbs ahead of the riders. The final climb was the First Category Col de Marie-Blanque, followed by 45 kilometres of descent and flat before the finish at Pau. Pedro Delgado won the stage but the stage was so tough, and the pace so fierce, that 17 riders abandoned the Tour altogether. The next morning two more riders quit, including Laurent Fignon.

❋ OUT BUT STILL IN ❋

Hippolyte Aucouturier, one of the favourites in the inaugural Tour de France of 1903, had to abandon Stage 1 because of stomach cramps. Today Aucouturier would be out of the Tour, but in early Tours a rider was allowed to race for stage wins even if he had failed to finish a previous stage. However, he was out of contention for the overall victory. In fact, Aucouturier won the second and third stages, from Lyon to Marseilles and Marseilles to Toulouse.

❋ SPAIN'S FIRST TOUR DE FRANCE WINNER ❋

In 1959 Federico Bahamontes became the first Spanish rider to win the Tour de France. When the race arrived in the Parc des Princes velodrome in Paris for the Tour's final metres, the peloton were greeted with derisive whistles. The crowd was unhappy that Jacques Anquetil and Roger Rivière, both members of the French national team, had conspired to deprive Henry Anglade, a French rider on the Centre-Midi regional team, of overall victory in favour of a Spanish rider. Anglade finished second in the race at 4 minutes 1 second while Anquetil was third overall and Rivière fourth. Bahamontes also won the King of the Mountains jersey, the third of six polka dot jerseys won in his career.

❋ A PIRATE REBOARDS SHIP ❋

In 2000, Marco Pantani (Mercatone Uno-Albacom) returned to professional racing when he entered and won two stages in the Tour de France. His mountain stage win on Mont Ventoux was controversial when Lance Armstrong appeared to ease back to allow "The Pirate" to take the stage victory. Pantani was incensed and told Armstrong that he was insulted by this gesture, which caused the pair to fall out.

❋ TOUR SPOKESMEN (18) ❋

"Gaul stood up on the pedals and, in the blink of an eye, he was 20 metres ahead. Then he disappeared round the next bend. The dark angel had passed; he fled in a cloud of dust."
Journalist Michel Claret, on Charly Gaul in 1958

❋ TOUR SCANDALS (2) ❋

After Michel Pollentier won the famous l'Alpe d'Huez stage of the 1978 Tour de France to claim the overall yellow jersey instead of making himself available for a urine sample, he went missing. When the Belgian rider eventually turned up two hours after claiming the stage victory, the medical team were somewhat suspicious of his earlier no-show. One doctor pulled up Pollentier's jersey to reveal a rubber bladder containing pre-prepared urine. He was immediately kicked out of the Tour and handed a two-year ban.

❋ TOUR SMALLEST MARGINS OF VICTORY ❋

Year	Winner	Margin	Runner-up
1989	Greg LeMond	at 8 seconds	Laurent Fignon
1968	Jans Janssen	at 38 seconds	Herman Van Springel
1987	Stephen Roche	at 40 seconds	Pedro Delgado
1977	Bernard Thévenet	at 48 seconds	Hennie Kuiper
1964	Jacques Anquetil	at 55 seconds	Raymond Poulidor
2006	Floyd Landis*	at 57 seconds	Oscar Pereiro

* Floyd Landis (USA) crossed the line first in 89h 39m 30s but was subsequently stripped of the winner's yellow jersey when he tested positive in a drugs test after winning Stage 17.

❋ APOLLO ON A BIKE ❋

The Swiss rider Hugo Koblet was an incredibly gifted rider who was nicknamed the Pédaleur de Charme (roughly translated as "beauty on a bike") because of his Greek god-like looks and superb riding ability. It was after his impressive "great escape" victory in Stage 11 of the 1951 Tour de France that the singer Jacques Grello coined the Pédaleur de Charme phrase. Born in Zurich, he was tall with undulating fair hair. *L'Equipe* called him "Apollo on a Bike". Koblet first made his name as a pursuit cyclist, winning the Swiss Championship in the discipline every year from 1947 to 1954. In 1947, he won the bronze medal at the World Championships and in 1951 he was offered a place as team leader on the Swiss team taking part in the Tour de France.

❋ THE KINGS OF THE MOUNTAINS ❋

Year	King of the Mountains	Country
1933	Vicente Trueba	Spain
1934	René Vietto	France
1935	Felicien Vervaecke	Belgium
1936	Julian Berrendero	Spain
1937	Felicien Vervaecke	Belgium
1938	Gino Bartali	Italy
1939	Sylvere Maes	Belgium
1947	Pierre Brambilla	Italy
1948	Gino Bartali	Italy
1949	Fausto Coppi	Italy
1950	Louison Bobet	France
1951	Raphaël Géminiani	France
1952	Fausto Coppi	Italy
1953	Jésus Lorono	Spain
1954	Federico Bahamontes	Spain
1955	Charly Gaul	Luxembourg
1956	Charly Gaul	Luxembourg
1957	Gastone Nencini	Italy
1958	Federico Bahamontes	Spain
1959	Federico Bahamontes	Spain
1960	Imerio Massigna	Italy
1961	Imerio Massignan	Italy
1962	Federico Bahamontes	Spain
1963	Federico Bahamontes	Spain
1964	Federico Bahamontes	Spain
1965	Julio Jimenez	Spain
1966	Julio Jimenez	Spain
1967	Julio Jimenez	Spain
1968	Aurelio Gonzalez	Spain
1969	Eddy Merckx	Belgium
1970	Eddy Merckx	Belgium
1971	Lucien Van Impe	Belgium
1972	Lucien Van Impe	Belgium
1973	Pedro Torres	Spain
1974	Domingo Perureña	Spain
1975	Lucien Van Impe	Belgium
1976	Giancarlo Bellini	Italy
1977	Lucien Van Impe	Belgium
1978	Mariano Martinez	France
1979	Giovanni Battaglin	Italy

1980	Raymond Martin	France
1981	Lucien Van Impe	Belgium
1982	Bernard Vallet	France
1983	Lucien Van Impe	Belgium
1984	Robert Millar	Great Britain
1985	Luis Herrera	Colombia
1986	Bernard Hinault	France
1987	Luis Herrera	Colombia
1988	Steven Rooks	Netherlands
1989	Gert-Jan Theunisse	Netherlands
1990	Thierry Claveyrolat	France
1991	Claudio Chiappucci	Italy
1992	Claudio Chiappucci	Italy
1993	Toni Rominger	Switzerland
1994	Richard Virenque	France
1995	Richard Virenque	France
1996	Richard Virenque	France
1997	Richard Virenque	France
1998	Christophe Rinero	France
1999	Richard Virenque	France
2000	Santiago Botero	Colombia
2001	Laurent Jalabert	France
2002	Laurent Jalabert	France
2003	Richard Virenque	France
2004	Richard Virenque	France
2005	Michael Rasmussen	Denmark
2006	Michael Rasmussen	Denmark
2007	Maurice Soler	Colombia
2008	No result*	
2009	No result*	
2010	Anthony Charteau	France
2011	Samuel Sanchez	Spain
2012	Thomas Voeckler	France

NOTES: * Two riders have been stripped of their titles by the UCI for doping offences: Italian Franco Pellizotti (2008) and Germany's Bernard Kohl (2009).

❊ PRETTY IN PINK AND YELLOW ❊

In 1964 Jacques Anquetil won his fourth consecutive Tour de France, becoming the first man to win the race five times. Having already won the pink jersey in the 1964 Giro d'Italia, he became only the second rider after Fausto Coppi to claim the two famous races in the same year. He also won Ghent–Wevelgem in 1964.

✻ GREAT TOURS DE FRANCE (5): 1955 ✻

Louison Bobet emulated Philippe Thys when he won his Tour de France and became the first rider to win three in a row. Bobet was assisted by a number of his French national teammates, notably Antonin Rolland, whose challenge ended as usual in the mountains. A great climber in his own right, Bobet took control of the yellow jersey on the first day in the Pyrenees, Stage 17. The King of the Mountains award, however, went to the man who would finish third overall, more than 11 minutes in arrears, Charly Gaul of Luxembourg. Separating Bobet and Gaul was a Belgian, Jean Brankart, almost five minutes behind the yellow jersey.

Rank	Name	Country	Time
1.	Louison Bobet	France	130h 29' 26"
2.	Jean Brankart	Belgium	+4' 53"
3.	Charly Gaul	Luxembourg	+11' 30"
4.	Pasquale Fornara	Italy	+12' 44"
5.	Antonin Rolland	France	+13' 18"
6.	Raphaël Géminiani	France	+15' 01"
7.	Giancarlo Astrua	Italy	+18' 13"
8.	Stan Ockers	Belgium	+27' 13"
9.	Alex Close	Belgium	+31' 10"
10.	François Mahé	France	+36' 27"

Did You Know That?
Miguel Poblet won the first and last stages of the 1955 Tour. The Spaniard managed only one other Tour stage victory, but he won the Tour of Spain and was national sprint, mountains and Madison champion during his 17-year career.

✻ VIVE LA FRANCE ✻

Up to and including the 2012 Tour de France, French riders have won the coveted overall *maillot jaune* the most number of times (36), followed by Belgium (18), Spain (12), United States (10), Italy (9), Luxembourg (5), Switzerland and the Netherlands (2 each) and Ireland, Denmark, Germany, Australia and Great Britain (1 each).

✻ TOUR SPOKESMEN (19) ✻

"He was total harmony, sublime, a phenomenon. He blended with his bicycle like a musician with his instrument."
Jacques Goddet, on Jacques Anquetil

❋ OLD LEATHERHEAD IS TOO LATE ❋

After Stage 20 of the 1959 Tour de France, which took place in the Alps, Jean "Old Leatherhead" Robic, winner of the first post-war Tour de France (1947), was eliminated for failing to make the stipulated time cut-off.

❋ LIGHTS GO OUT ON MERCKX ❋

Late in 1969, after Eddy Merckx had won his inaugural Tour de France, he had a terrible crash in a derny-paced race. The race took place at night under floodlights when suddenly the electricity went out, causing Merckx and Fernand Wambst, his derny pacer, to crash on the velodrome in Blois, France. Wambst died and Merckx suffered a cracked vertebra. The injury caused Merckx back problems for the remainder of his career and in some Tour film footage, Merckx can be seen adjusting his saddle in the middle of a race in an attempt to find some relief from the pain he was suffering, particularly in the mountains.

❋ UNDISPUTED KING OF THE MOUNTAINS ❋

Richard Virenque (France) won King of the Mountains a record seven times: in 1994, 1995, 1996, 1997, 1999, 2003 and 2004.

❋ PRIM AND PROPER ❋

Just as he was to do in Stage 11 of the 1951 Tour de France, on the hardest climb of the 1950 Tour of Switzerland Hugo Koblet (Switzerland) took the trouble to comb his hair, aiming to earn a psychological advantage over his rivals by giving the impression that it was all too easy. In reality Koblet was suffering with haemorrhoids but the ruse fooled his rival François Mahé, who gave up trying to stay with him. Koblet went on to win the Tour of Switzerland.

❋ THE FIRST TOUR HAT-TRICK ❋

In 1920 Philippe Thys (Belgium) did what no other rider in the history of the Tour de France was able to accomplish before him: win the world's most prestigious bike race for a record third time. His feat would not be matched again until the 1953, 1954 and 1955 triple victories of Frenchman Louison Bobet.

❋ MAN AT C&A ❋

Stage 8 of the 1978 Tour de France was a 59.3-kilometre individual time trial won by 23-year-old Bernard Hinault, who beat Eddy Merckx's former right-hand man and good friend Joseph Bruyère by 34 seconds and Freddy Maertens by almost a minute. Bruyère of the C&A team was now in yellow and Hinault had lifted himself to fourth place in the general classification. Hinault went on to win the 1978 Tour de France.

❋ TOUR SPOKESMEN (20) ❋

"If by some chance I don't win the Tour he won't win it either."
Jacques Anquetil, on Raymond Poulidor in 1966, the year Lucien Aimar won

❋ MERCKX GIVES AWAY HIS GREEN JERSEY ❋

At the final awards ceremony in Paris for the 1972 Tour de France, Cyrille Guimard presented the green sprinter's jersey to Eddy Merckx, who had just won his fourth consecutive Tour. Merckx, however, gave it back to Guimard, who was in tears, telling him that it was really his. On Stage 17 of the 1972 Tour, Guimard, who was lying in second place in the overall general classification (at 6 minutes 20 seconds to Merckx) and had won several stages in the race, fell off his bike twice during a climb and on the Ballon d'Alsace. Despite having to be placed under constant medical attention for the remainder of that stage, he struggled to the finish line that day. However, the next day he was forced to abandon the Tour after just 10 kilometres of Stage 18, the penultimate stage.

1972 Points Competition:
1. Eddy Merckx: 196 points
2. Rik Van Linden: 135 points
3. Joop Zoetemelk: 132 points

❋ A FAMOUS LUNCH ❋

In November 1902, Henri Desgrange and Géo Lefèvre had lunch in a Parisian restaurant called Zimmer (today it's a TGI Friday's restaurant). It was Lefèvre who first proposed the idea of a race on roads all round France to Desgrange. However, Desgrange claimed the idea as his own and started the inaugural Tour de France the following year.

✵ STAGE WINNER IN DISNEYLAND ✵

Australia's Stuart O'Grady snatched victory from Italy's Giuseppe Calcaterra on the finish line in Stage 14 of the 1998 Tour de France, a 186.5km ride from Valréas to Grenoble. The 24-year-old, who had worn the *maillot jaune* for three days earlier in the race, was so pleased with his victory that he described being in the Tour as "just like being in Disneyland". Calcaterra was later relegated to sixth place in the stage standings after moving into O'Grady on the line, while the Portuguese rider Orlando Rodrigues was awarded second place.

✵ THE GREATEST-EVER STAGE FINISH ✵

Many Tour de France fans consider Stage 21 of the 1987 Tour to be the greatest-ever in the history of the race. The stage began with Pedro Delgado in yellow at 25 seconds from Stephen Roche. In November 2003, Roche gave an interview to *Cycle Sport* magazine about that fateful day: "I had the jersey at Villard-de-Lans (Stage 19, won by Delgado). But Delgado took it back from me the next day at the summit of l'Alpe d'Huez (Stage 20). I was not a climber like him. Between the descent of the Galibier and the foot of the Madeleine (Stage 21) I attacked because he was isolated. I passed him and rejoined the group ahead. Afterwards I climbed the Madeleine alone. Delgado and his teammates caught me again at the foot of La Plagne. I said to myself, 'What am I going to do? If I stay with him he'll kill me. I'll never get to the top. I let him go and conceded 1'10, 1'15. But he didn't trust himself. And four kilometres from the line, I attacked at top speed. I gave it everything I had. And I got to within a few seconds of him. Psychologically, that was my most beautiful victory." Roche collapsed at the finish line and was given oxygen and taken to hospital, but he was later found to be fine. The GC now showed Roche trailing Delgado by 39 seconds after the Irishman was penalised 10 seconds for taking an illegal feed. Roche went on to win the 1987 Tour de France, becoming the first and only Irishman to do so.

✵ THE CANNIBAL LOSES HIS APPETITE ✵

The 1977 Tour de France was Eddy Merckx's last. He finished in sixth place overall at 12 minutes 38 seconds behind the winner Bernard Thévenet (Peugeot-Esso). In 1978, Merckx rode in only five events, but didn't enjoy a victory. The Cannibal finally lost his appetite after taking part in some 1,800 races and winning more than 500 of them.

✻ TOUR LEGENDS (5) – BERNARD THEVENET ✻

Bernard Thévenet was born into a farming family on 10 January 1948 in Saint-Julien-de-Civry, Saône-et-Loire, France. Cycling captured his imagination after his sister placed him on her bike's handlebars and cycled 5km to school. He got his own bike aged seven and cycled to school on it.

Thévenet was a choirboy in 1961 when he first saw the Tour de France in 1961. "The priest brought forward the time for Mass so that we could watch the riders go by," he recalled. "They were modern-day knights. I had already been dreaming of becoming a racing cyclist and that magical sight convinced me definitively. It was never that magical when I was actually in the peloton of the Tour!"

Despite needing help on the farm, his parents realised that Bernard wanted to be a professional cyclist and bought him a racing bike as a reward for passing his school exams. Thévenet was Burgundy Champion in 1965 and 1966 and, in 1967, joined the prestigious Boulogne-Billancourt club, becoming the 1968 Junior French Champion. After turning professional with Peugeot, he rode in his first Tour in 1970, winning Stage 18. A year later he won a second Tour stage and finished fourth overall.

In the 1972 Tour, Thévenet won two more stages and finished ninth overall. Bernard won his only French Road Race Championship title in 1973 and finished second overall behind Spain's Luis Ocaña, in the Tour, winning two more stages. He also finished third in the 1973 Vuelta a España. France's hopes for a first home Tour winner since 1967 were high in 1974, but Thévenet had to abandon. A year later, however, he ended five-time winner Eddy Merckx's domination by winning the *maillot jaune*. Thévenet also won the Critérium du Dauphiné in 1975 and retained that title in 1976, though he abandoned on Stage 19 of the Tour.

Thévenet won his second Tour in three years in 1977 and what proved to be his ninth and last stage victory. Sadly, the defending champion abandoned the 1978 Tour after Stage 11. In 1979 Bernard signed for the Spanish team, Teka, staying with them for two years. After missing the Tour in 1979 – he did finish 31st in the Giro d'Italia – Thévenet finished 17th in 1980. Bernard joined the Puch Wobler Campagnolo team for the 1981 season, and finished 37th overall in his final Tour.

He was appointed *directeur sportif* of the La Redoute team in 1984, which included future Tour winner Stephen Roche. In 1986 he became *directeur sportif* of the RMO team and later became a television commentator.

Did You Know That?
Bernard Thévenet's family lived in a hamlet called Le Guidon (The Handlebar).

❋ DENMARK'S FIRST ❋

Bjarne Riis (Denmark, Telekom), who had finished third in the 1995 Tour de France, became the first, and to date only Danish rider to win the world's greatest cycle race when he won the 1996 Tour.

❋ GOING THE WRONG WAY ❋

Marcel Molines (Algeria) won Stage 13 of the 1950 Tour de France from Perpignan to Nîmes but his victory was not the biggest news story of the day. Abdel Khader Zaaf, his colleague in the North African team comprising riders from Algeria and Morocco, broke away along with Molines about 15 kilometres into the stage. Less than 20 kilometres from the finish Zaaf began to wobble on his bike, zigzagging across the road. On noticing his erratic riding and concerned for his overall safety, a race official stopped him from going any further, but after a brief rest Zaaf claimed he was fine and remounted his bike before falling off and apparently falling asleep at the side of the road. When he was woken he got back on his bike and started to race down the road in the wrong direction. He was stopped again by a race official and an ambulance was called for him. After Molines rode to victory, Zaaf claimed that when a spectator woke him up he gave him a drink of wine. Zaaf was a devout Muslim unfamiliar with alcohol but when the ambulance crew found his pulse to be 160, and pumped his stomach, they were of the opinion that Zaaf's condition had been brought on by a combination of drugs, exhaustion and dehydration.

❋ THE LAST OF THE BREED ❋

By the time the 1978 Tour de France came around, the famous Merckx–Thévenet era was over despite the fact that Thévenet, winner in 1975 and again in 1977, would continue to ride the Tour until 1981; 1978, however, marked the beginning of the dominance of the race by *"Le Blaireau"* ("The Badger"), Bernard Hinault. Hinault, winner that year, the first of his five Tour victories, was an all-rounder: he was able to climb, sprint and time trial. He raced the classics, stage races, national and world championships and won them all. He truly was the last of this breed of "complete" rider.

❋ THE BIRTH OF THE UCI WORLD CUP ❋

The Super Prestige Pernod International was raced from 1961–
1987 and was the forerunner to the UCI World Cup. The race
was won by many cycling legends including Jacques Anquetil,
the inaugural winner and a three-times winner overall, and Eddy
Merckx who holds the record for the highest number of wins with
seven consecutive victories from 1969–1975. In 1987 the French
government introduced a ban on sports sponsorship by alcohol
brands, including Pernod. In 1988, the competition was replaced by
the UCI World Cup and in its early years was sponsored by Perrier.

❋ DUTCH TOUR WINNERS ❋

1 1 win...Jan Janssen (1968)
= 1 win...Joop Zoetemelk (1980)

❋ CLIMBERS RECOGNISED BY THE TOUR ❋

In 1933, Tour boss Henri Desgrange introduced the "King of the
Mountains" classification with Spaniard Vicente Trueba its first
winner. The following year Desgrange made it an official category,
with France's René Vietto the winner. The polka dot jersey, however,
wasn't introduced until 1975. The jersey's sponsor was chocolate
maker Poulain, whose wrappers incorporated polka dots. The Dutch
rider Joop Zoetemelk was the first to wear the now famous jersey,
after claiming it in the 1975 Prologue.

❋ THE SIX-STAGE TOUR DE FRANCE ❋

The first Tour de France, held in 1903, comprised six days of racing
with a rest-day in between each stage.

❋ AN EXPENSIVE GUARANTEE ❋

In 1903, with just a week to go before the start of the inaugural
Tour de France, only 15 riders were signed up. To boost interest
in the race Henri Desgrange decided to shorten and reschedule it
from a 31 May start and 5 July ending to a 1 July start and 18 July
finish. He also promised five francs a day in expenses to the first 50
riders who signed up, and an overall 20,000-franc guaranteed prize
money purse. Desgrange's financial incentive worked, and 60 riders
signed up.

✽ SPEEDY TEAM ✽

In 1995, Gewiss set the fastest-ever team time trial in the Tour, 54.930 kph over 67km.

✽ TOUR SPOKESMEN (21) ✽

"I always had and still have that special desire in me to be the best. That's why I accept, and why I am proud of, the nickname they once gave me: The Cannibal."
Eddy Merckx, five-time winner of the Tour de France

✽ FIRST MOUNTAIN TIME TRIAL ✽

The 1939 Tour de France had a total of five individual time trials. One of them was the Tour's first-ever mountain time trial, up the 2,770-metre-high Col d'Iseran. Sylvère Maes (Belgium) displayed his mastery of the bike by winning the 64.5-kilometre hill climb, taking 4 minutes out of Ward Vissers (Belgium) and 10 minutes out of René Vietto (France South-East). Maes went on to win the yellow jersey in a time of 132 hours 3 minutes 17 seconds and the King of the Mountains title (86 points).

✽ IT'S MY RACE ✽

In 1908 Henri Desgrange stated that riders had to race on bike frames provided by the organisers of the Tour. The frames were allowed to be constructed using some components chosen by the rider, but ultimately Desgrange was attempting to reduce the influence of the riders' sponsors, with whom he had a love-hate relationship.

✽ THE *DOMESTIQUE* IS BORN ✽

When Henri Desgrange learned that Maurice Brocco (France) had helped François Faber (Luxembourg) finish Stage 8 of the 1911 Tour de France, he was furious but unable to kick him out of the race. Desgrange believed in fair play above all, and that all riders should ride in the Tour alone without help from anyone. In an article written by Desgrange for *L'Auto*, he called Brocco unworthy and nothing more than a *domestique* (servant). Today the term *domestique* is used to describe a rider in a team who is there to assist the team leader and plays a key role in the team.

❋ WHAT'S YOUR NAME? ❋

In the first-ever Tour peloton in 1903, some riders raced under a pseudonym. Julien Lootens raced the inaugural Tour de France as "Samson" while Lucien Mazan raced as "Petit-Breton".

❋ GAUL'S OBSCENE GESTURE ❋

Louison Bobet (France), winner of the Tour de France in 1953, 1954 and 1955, was too exhausted to compete in the 1957 race. During the 1957 Giro d'Italia several riders including Bobet, Charly Gaul (1956 Giro winner) and Gastone Nencini stopped for a toilet break. Bobet and Nencini remounted and continued riding without waiting for Gaul, who was at the time wearing the leader's pink jersey. According to reports Gaul then made an indecent gesture at Bobet, and thus began a war between the two. An enraged Gaul rode like a man possessed that day and placed Nencini in the pink at the end of the stage. The following day Bobet decided he was racing for the lead and when his team attacked, they had Gaul and Nencini with them. Nencini fell behind the leaders after he flatted, as Bobet raced ahead gaining time all the way. However, Gaul waited for Nencini and paced the Italian up the remaining climbs, preferring to sacrifice his own placing rather than let Bobet win the Giro. Gaul's plan worked as they clawed back time on Bobet, which meant Nencini remained in pink and went on to win the 1957 Giro. Bobet had given everything he had in the race, and his efforts left him so exhausted that he opted out of the 1957 Tour de France.

❋ TOUR SPOKESMEN (22) ❋

"I got my teammates together and told them I would go for the victory. I would take the yellow jersey in the mountains or drop in the attempt. It was this year or never."
Bernard Thévenet, Tour de France winner in 1975 and 1977

❋ TRAIN HOPPERS ❋

Several riders were kicked out of the 1906 Tour de France after it was discovered that they took the train rather than ride up the Ballon d'Alsace. René Pottier (France) won the stage in a 200-kilometre solo breakaway and finished 47 minutes ahead of his nearest competitor. Many regarded the 1906 Tour de France winner as the first-ever great King of the Mountains, such was his mastery of climbing.

✳ ITALIANS BURY THE HATCHET ✳

Stage 12 of the 1952 Tour de France included four climbs in the Maritime Alps. When the yellow jersey leader Fausto Coppi got a puncture – incredibly he suffered three flat tyres in a 20-kilometre stretch of road in one day – Gino Bartali generously gave his teammate and team leader his wheel. The long rivalry between the two had finally come to an end. Coppi won the 1952 Tour.

✳ BLIND BUT NOT WITHOUT VISION ✳

On Stage 5 of the 1949 Tour de France, Fausto Coppi (Italy) broke away with the yellow jersey of Jacques Marinelli (France) and five others. Suddenly, with a six-minute lead over the chasing peloton, a roadside fan caused Marinelli and Coppi to crash. Marinelli was unhurt and his bike was undamaged so he continued the race; however, the unhurt Coppi's bike was wrecked, and when he was offered a replacement from the Italian team car which wasn't his own personal spare, he refused to accept it and threatened to quit the Tour unless his own bike was found. When his teammate Gino Bartali caught up with him, he decided to wait with Coppi until the acceptable replacement bike arrived. Some time later the Italian team manager Alfredo Binda turned up with Coppi's replacement bike, and both Bartali and Coppi rode off in pursuit of the leading riders in the stage. However Coppi began to slow, complaining of hunger and exhaustion, and Bartali felt he was left with no other choice but to chase down the leaders alone. When Coppi finally crossed the stage finish line he had lost over 18 minutes. Following the stage Coppi complained to Binda that he was showing favouritism by not following him when he was in the leading pack of racers, and made it clear that he was unwilling to ride for a team in which Bartali received a higher level of team support. Binda was then left with the difficult task of massaging Coppi's ego and convincing his rider that he was not favouring one rider over another, explaining that he had been delayed in reaching Coppi with his replacement bike. The popular story goes that Coppi finally accepted Binda's explanation when a blind man walked into the room with his guide dog as the pair were arguing. The blind man walked up to the pair and told Coppi that he had named his dog Fausto and that he would never betray his dog and his dog would never betray him. On hearing this, Coppi took stock of the situation and decided to accept Binda's story. Despite being over 36 minutes behind the yellow jersey of Marinelli, Coppi went on to win the 1949 Tour de France.

❋ GREAT CLIMBS (5) – COL DE LA MADELEINE ❋

The Col de la Madeleine was not crossed by the Tour de France until 1969, but such is the challenge that the organisers have made it a staple ever since and it has now appeared 24 times. It has been conquered by many of the great climbers of Tour history and both Lucien Van Impe and Richard Virenque, the only six-time King of the Mountains, have led the field over the top of the Madeleine on three occasions. On the first *hors catégorie* climb of Stage 11 in 2012, no fewer than 28 riders broke away and led the peloton by almost three minutes.

Location: The département of Savoie and region of Rhône-Alpes in eastern France.

Nearest town: Celliers.

Height: The peak is at 2,000m, but Tour points are awarded at 1,993m.

Gradient: This climb covers 24.54km and rises 1,543m, an average gradient of 6.3 percent. However, the gradient is 10 percent from 12km to 17km and 8.0 up the final 4.5km.

Characteristics: The road to the top of the Col de la Madeleine climbs 24km out of a valley on a twisting road which gives the impression of tiers around a wedding cake. The view at the summit – not that the riders stop for such things – is stunning and spectacular.

Tour visits: 24.

Multiple winners:
3: Lucien Van Impe   (1979, 1981, 1983)
    Richard Virenque   (1995, 1996, 1997)

Conquerors of the peak: Andres Ganarias (1969), Jean-Pierre Danguillaume (1973), Francisco Galdos (1975), André Chalmel (1977), Mariano Martinez (1980), Pedro Delgado (1984), Anselmo Fuerte (1987), Henri Abadie (1988), Thierry Claveyrolat (1990), Piotr Ugrumov (1994), Jan Ullrich (1998), Massimilano Lelli (2000), Laurent Roux (2001), Michael Boogerd (2002), Gilberto Simoni (2004), Santiago Botero (2005), Anthony Charteau (2010), Peter Velits (2012).

Did You Know That?
At the end of the Col de la Madeleine stage in the 2012 Tour (Stage 11), there was a first-ever British one-two in the general classification, Bradley Wiggins leading Chris Froome.

✳ LeMOND HANDS HINAULT STAGE WIN ✳

Stage 18 of the 1986 Tour de France included climbs up the Col du Galiber, the Télégraphe, the Croix de Fer and finally a hilltop finish at l'Alpe d'Huez. Greg LeMond, in yellow, and his La Vie Claire teammate Bernard Hinault were the first riders to reach the top of l'Alpe d'Huez and as the pair approached the line, the young American sportingly took Hinault's hand and let the five-times Tour de France winner claim the stage victory.

✳ MARATHON STAGE ✳

Stage 6 of the 1920 Tour de France over the Pyrenees took winner Firmin Lambot (Belgium) over 15 hours to complete.

✳ COURAGEOUS EDDY ✳

Eddy Merckx (Molteni) crashed early on Stage 16 of the 1975 Tour de France but despite being bloodied and in severe pain, he got back on his bike and finished third in the stage. When the doctor examined Merckx afterwards, it was discovered that he had broken both his cheekbone and his jaw. Most men would have abandoned the Tour there and then, but Merckx was no ordinary man. He refused to give up his dream of claiming a record sixth Tour and continued racing despite the fact that he could only take liquid food. Merckx finished runner-up in the 1975 Tour at 2 minutes 47 seconds behind Bernard Thévenet (Peugeot-BP).

✳ LEADING RIDER FALLS OFF HIS BIKE ✳

Robert Jacquinot won Stage 5 of the 1923 Tour de France and the next day's Stage 6 covered 326 kilometres with the riders having to cross the Aubisque, the Tourmalet, the Aspin and the Peyresourde. When Jacquinot, who looked certain to win the stage and claim the yellow jersey, reached the 1,569-metre Peyresourde he was so exhausted that he fell off his bike. Although he managed to get back in the saddle, Jean Alavoine rode past him and took the stage win, 16 minutes in front of Jacquinot.

❋ NO TEAM GAME ❋

After a two-year trial, whereby each team in the Tour was a national team, the Tour reverted to trade teams in 1969. Jan Janssen (Holland) won the 1968 Tour de France in 133 hours, 49 minutes and 42 seconds.

❋ A DOPEY RIDER ❋

After Stage 8 of the 1968 Tour de France, the French "A" team rider José Samyn had the dubious distinction of being the first rider to be kicked out of the Tour for failing doping controls.

❋ CHAMPAGNE JACQUES ❋

Folklore has it that when Jacques Anquetil (St Raphaël-Gitane) was struggling in the mountains on Stage 14 of the 1964 Tour de France, he considered quitting the race before reinvigorating himself with a flask of champagne. Before the race a psychic had predicted that Anquetil would abandon the Tour on the fourteenth stage following an accident. After Stage 13 Anquetil went to a barbecue where he ate and drank well, and perhaps the alcohol allowed the psychic's prediction to play on his mind. At any rate by the top of the Port d'Envalira, Anquetil was 4 minutes behind the leaders and the story goes that Raphaël Géminiani, Anquetil's race director, drove up close to him and gave him the flask containing champagne. Anquetil then rode furiously and caught the leading group to cross the finishing line alongside them. He was now second overall in the GC at 1 minutes 26 seconds behind Georges Groussard (Pelforth).

❋ A BELATED GIFT ❋

The yellow jersey was not awarded to the 1920 Tour's leader until Philippe Thys (Belgium) won Stage 9.

❋ BROKEN WHEEL, BROKEN DREAM ❋

During Stage 6 of the 1922 Tour de France, which took the riders into the Pyrenees and over the Aubisque, the Aspin and the Peyresourde, three-times winner Philippe Thys (Belgium) lost three and a half hours because of a broken wheel, thus ending his chances of a fourth victory.

❋ TOUR SPOKESMEN (23) ❋

"I won! I won! I don't have to go to school any more."
Eddy Merckx, after winning his first bike race

❋ BIG MIG WINS FIVE ON THE TROT ❋

In 1995, Miguel Indurain made it five consecutive Tour de France wins. Amazingly Big Mig won his five Tours without ever winning a single road stage. His 12 stage victories were all individual time trials.

❋ THE MONSTER TOUR ❋

In 1937, the new Tour de France race organiser Jacques Goddet introduced 31 stages into the 26 days of the Tour. On three separate occasions, the riders had to ride three stages in a single day.

❋ A COSTLY BIKE CHANGE ❋

During Stage 9 of the 1907 Tour de France from Toulouse to Bayonne, Emile Georget crashed at a checkpoint and his Peugeot teammate, Pierre-Gonzague Privat, gave him his bike to continue racing. This was contrary to Desgrange's strict rule that a rider must start and finish each stage with the same bike, but Desgrange was reluctant to eliminate one of the Tour's star riders whose adventures helped sell papers, and so after receiving a severe points penalty Georget was placed third in the GC. At the time a fierce rivalry existed between Georget's team (Peugeot) and Louis Trousselier's Alcyon team. Alcyon was unhappy with the points penalty given to Georget and claimed he should have been kicked out of the Tour altogether, and when Desgrange disagreed with them, they withdrew from the Tour completely. This was the first time a team had pulled out of the Tour de France, but it was not to be the last.

❋ THE FIRST-EVER STAGE ❋

Maurice Garin, riding the red, white and blue tricolour bike of his sponsor *La Française*, won the inaugural stage of the inaugural Tour de France in 1903, beating Emile Pagie by 55 seconds. The first stage was 467 kilometres long and took the riders from Paris to Lyon, a muscle-sapping 17 hours 45 minutes of riding both day and night. Garin held the lead throughout the Tour.

❋ BROKEN DREAMS ❋

René Vietto (France) quit the 1936 Tour de France on Stage 6 after suffering two broken chains.

❋ COUNTING THE DOTS ❋

With seven polka dot jerseys (1994, 1995, 1996, 1997, 1999. 2003 and 2004), France's Richard Virenque is indisputably the greatest climber the Tour de France has ever seen. However, two other riders have won the King of the Mountains title six times:

Rider	Nationality	Years
Federico Bahamontes	Spain	1954, 1958, 1959, 1962, 1963, 1964
Lucien Van Impe	Belgian	1971, 1972, 1975, 1977, 1981, 1983

❋ MERCKX BEATEN ON HOME TURF ❋

Stage 7 of the 1970 Tour de France took the race into the Brussels suburb of Forest, with the home favourite Eddy Merckx wearing the leader's yellow jersey. However, the afternoon's short time trial produced a shock result when Jose Gonzales-Linares, the Spanish champion, beat Merckx by 3 seconds on the 7.2-kilometre course. Merckx did retain the yellow jersey and went on to win the Tour.

❋ CANNIBAL CLIMBS IZOARD FOR FIRST TIME ❋

Stage 13 of the 1972 Tour de France, from Orcières Merlette to Briançon taking in the Vars and Izoard mountains, was the first time Eddy Merckx, who was wearing the yellow jersey, had ridden over the Izoard. Merckx took the historical stage victory.

❋ A PLAYBOY LIFESTYLE ❋

In 1965 Jacques Anquetil won the eight-day Alpine Critérium du Dauphiné Libéré stage race at 3pm, then for the following two hours he was interviewed by television and the press before boarding a private jet at 6.30pm for a flight to Bordeaux. The following day, according to many after one of his famous all-night drinking and card-playing sessions, he won the world's longest single-day classic, the Bordeaux–Paris. Several cycling commentators claim, and few people have denied, that the private jet laid on to get Anquetil to Bordeaux was paid for out of government funds at the behest of President Charles de Gaulle.

❋ GREAT TOURS DE FRANCE (6): 1964 ❋

Two Tour legends went head-to-head during the 1964 Tour de France: winner Jacques Anquetil and his compatriot Raymond Poulidor. Their epic battle on Stage 20, from Brive up to the Puy de Dôme, remains an iconic contest, the photograph of them side-by-side on the lung-bursting climb starkly reminding everyone just how tough the Tour is. The two riders were separated by 55 seconds in Paris – at the time the closest-ever margin – but things might have been different had Poulidor remembered that on Stage 9, in Monaco, riders would pass the finishing point twice. Poulidor burst clear the first time and led everyone over the line; when it mattered Anquetil took the stage, together with the one-minute bonus.

Rank	Name	Country	Time
1.	Jacques Anquetil	France	127h 09' 44"
2.	Raymond Poulidor	France	+55"
3.	Federico Bahamontes	Spain	+4' 44"
4.	Henry Anglade	France	+6' 42"
5.	Georges Groussard	France	+10' 34"
6.	André Foucher	France	+10' 36"
7.	Julio Jiminez	Spain	+12' 13"
8.	Gilbert Desmet	Belgium	+12' 17"
9.	Hans Junkermann	Germany	+14' 02"
10.	Vittorio Adorni	Italy	+14' 19"

Did You Know That?
As well as becoming the Tour's first five-time winner, Anquetil emulated Italy's Fausto Coppi in winning the Giro d'Italia and Tour de France in the same year.

❋ CHAMPION OF CHAMPIONS ❋

In 1970 Eddy Merckx repeated his 1969 Tour victory. He won his second successive Tour de France after a superb season which saw him capture the Het Volk, Paris–Roubaix, Paris–Nice and the Giro d'Italia, and when he arrived at the 1970 Tour de France he was proudly sporting his new Belgian Road Champion's jersey.

❋ TOUR SPOKESMEN (24) ❋

"Today is the greatest moment in my whole life."
Greg LeMond, on winning the Tour de France in 1989

✵ THE LANGUAGE OF THE TOUR ✵

Here is a selection of the French terms used in the Tour and their translation.

Attaquer	To attack
Autobus	A group of riders who work together to finish inside the time limit
Bidon	Water bottle
Bonification	Time bonus
Casque	Helmet
Chute	Crash
Classement	Classification
Col	Mountain pass
Commissaire	Race official
Contre-la-montre	Time trial (individual or team)
Coureurs groupés	Sponsored riders
Coureurs isolés	Self-sufficient individual riders
Crevaison	Puncture
Départ fictif	Neutral start, from here riders don't race, but their speed is controlled by a lead car
Départ réel	The end of the part of the stage from Départ fictif, after which the riders race as normal
Directeur sportif	Team manager
Domestique	Support rider in a team
Dossard	Attachment a rider wears displaying his race number
Échappé	Breakaway on a stage
Équipe	Team
Étape	Stage of a tour
Flamme rouge	Red flag denoting one kilometre left on a stage
Grand Boucle	The Tour de France route, literally the "big loop"
Grimpeur	Specialist mountain climber
Hors-catégorie	The hardest mountain climb, literally "beyond classification"
Lanterne rouge	"Red light", the last-placed rider in the general classification
Maillot à pois	Polka dot jersey, worn by the King of the Mountains leader
Maillot blanc	White jersey, worn by the leading rider aged 25 or under
Maillot jaune	Yellow jersey, worn by the overall Tour leader
Maillot vert	Green jersey, worn by the points competition (sprints) leader

Musette..Feed bag
Parcours...The route
Pavé...Cobbled roads
Peloton...The main body of riders
Piste...In this case, a cycle track
Pneu..Tyre
Pneu crevé...Flat tyre
Poinçonnées..............................Unsponsored riders of the 1900s
Primé.....A point along a Tour route where there is a subsidiary prize
Pursuivant................................Rider chasing the leader on the road
Randonée............Leisure ride, which may be timed, but is not a race
Ravitaillement...Feed zone
Roue...Wheel
Rouleur.............Rider strongest on long, rolling or flat stages
Soigneur...........Team assistant who does everything: massaging riders,
              doing their laundry and preparing their food and drink
Tête de course...The stage leader
Touriste-routier ....1930s-era rider who didn't
                                        compete as a professional
Voiture balai............The broom wagon, which picks up any rider who
              abandons the race or falls too far behind on a stage

❋ A BLOODY FACE ❋

On Stage 15 of the 1968 Tour de France, a motorcycle swerved
to avoid a spectator and caught Raymond Poulidor's (France "A"
team) handlebars and brought the rider down. Poulidor remounted
and raced on with a broken nose, finishing a heroic ride with blood
splattered all over his face just 4 minutes 3 seconds behind his
teammate and stage winner, Roger Pingeon.

❋ CAMERADERIE ❋

André Leducq (France) was the dominant rider in the 1932 Tour de
France, winning six stages, as well as claiming two second- and three
third-place finishes out of the 21 stages on his way to winning the
overall yellow jersey. However, things could have been very different
had his teammate Georges Speicher not given Leducq a wheel from
his own bike when Leducq flatted in the mountains. Leducq's superb
performance in the saddle earned him 31 minutes in bonuses, while
Kurt Stoepel (Germany), the runner-up, had earned 7 bonus minutes,
a 24-minute difference. Leducq won the Tour by 24 minutes 3 seconds
from the German. The Italians won seven of the 21 stages in 1932.

✻ TOUR LEGENDS (6) – BERNARD HINAULT ✻

Bernard Hinault was born on 14 November 1954 in Yffiniac, Brittany, France. He began his professional cycling career in 1974, starting a close relationship with Cyrille Guimard, the *directeur sportif* of the Gitane team. In 1977 Hinault won the Grand Prix des Nations, the Critérium du Dauphiné Libéré and Liège–Bastogne–Liège but did not enter any of the grand tours, opting to fully prepare for the 1978 season. It was an inspired decision as Hinault, now riding for Renault-Elf-Gitane, made his debuts in both the Tour de France and Vuelta a España, winning both, as well as a second Grand Prix des Nations.

Hinault successfully defended his *maillot jaune* in 1979 and a third consecutive Grand Prix des Nations, second Critérium du Dauphiné Libéré, the Giro di Lombardia and La Flèche Wallonne. His hopes of a Tour hat-trick in 1980 were ended by a knee injury, but he was back in 1981, winning his third Tour, four stages, the combination classification and the combativity award. In 1982 Hinault claimed the Tour–Giro double following victory in the Giro d'Italia.

The following year, 1983, Hinault once again was forced to miss the Tour de France through a knee injury. He was back in 1984, when he finished runner-up behind the defending champion Laurent Fignon. However, following disagreements with Guimard in 1983 he had left the Renault team and signed for La Vie Claire, who had Swiss coach Paul Koechli as *directeur sportif*. Koechli taught Hinault meditation and relaxation methods and these helped him equal the legendary Jacques Anquetil's feat of winning five overall Tours.

Many years after that 1985 Tour, Hinault's teammate Greg LeMond claimed that La Vie Claire had lied to him about his lead over Hinault during a mountain stage, thus forcing him to wait on Hinault, which effectively cost the American his first Tour victory. The Frenchman and American fought an aggressive Tour de France in 1986, which went LeMond's way.

Hinault retired from professional cycling after the 1986 Tour and returned to farming in Brittany before later becoming involved with the Tour organisation. His 28 Tour stage wins and a total of 75 days in the *maillot jaune* rank second behind only Eddy Merckx in both categories. He is also one of the few men to win points (1979) and King of the Mountains (1986) crowns as well as the overall classification. Overall, Hinault won more than 200 events in his 12-year professional career.

Did You Know That?
In 1978, Hinault successfully led a riders' protest against split stages in the Tour, whereby the cyclists rode stages in the morning and afternoon.

❋ TOUR SPOKESMEN (25) ❋

"I am ready to cope with fame."
Laurent Fignon, *winner of the Tour de France in 1983 and 1984*

❋ UNLUCKY STAGE 13 ❋

Stage 13 of the 1951 Tour de France, from Dax to Tarbes, included both the Tourmalet and the Aubisque. Wim Van Est (Holland) was in yellow but suffered a flat tyre near the top of the Aubisque. When he remounted he joined Fiorenzo Magni (winner of the Giro d'Italia in 1948, 1951 and 1955) and tried to hold on to the Italian's wheel on the descent before crashing, remounting and continuing down the mountain. When he went too fast into a decreasing radius turn he lost control of his bike and flew off the side of the cliff, ending up 20 metres below. Luckily for Van Est his fall was broken by trees, which prevented him from falling further. Mechanics and riders looked down the ravine and could see Van Est waving his arms, but there were no ropes available to lower down to him. Instead they made a rope from tubular tyres and lowered a person down the cliff face to rescue him. When he was finally hauled to safety his only concern was for his bike, as he wanted to resume the race. However the brave Dutchman was forced to go to hospital for an examination that revealed only bruises and scratches. With his Tour over, the entire Dutch team quit the race in solidarity.

❋ ERIN GO BRAGH ❋

In 1987, Stephen Roche (Ireland) won the Giro d'Italia, the Tour de France and the World Road Cycling Championship. Amazingly only one other rider in the history of the sport, Eddy Merckx (Belgium), has been able to win this coveted hat-trick in one year.

❋ SPECTATOR ENDS SINKEWITZ'S TOUR ❋

During the 2007 Tour de France Germany's Patrik Sinkewitz, part of the T-Mobile team, was forced to withdraw from the race after colliding with a spectator.

✵ BELGIAN TOUR WINNERS ✵

1	5 wins	Eddy Merckx (1969, 1970, 1971, 1972, 1974)
2	3 wins	Philippe Thys (1913, 1914, 1920)
3	2 wins	Firmin Lambot (1919, 1922)
=	2 wins	Sylvère Maes (1936, 1939)
5	1 win	Odile Defraye (1912)
=	1 win	Léon Scieur (1921)
=	1 win	Lucien Buysse (1926)
=	1 win	Maurice De Waele (1929)
=	1 win	Romain Maes (1935)
=	1 win	Lucien Van Impe (1976)

✵ ALWAYS THE BRIDESMAID ✵

Many sports writers agree that had it not been for Jacques Anquetil's domination of the Tour de France during the early 1960s, Raymond Poulidor would surely have won the race at least once. Poulidor was a vastly superior climber to Anquetil (the master time trialler and race tactician) but he was never able to gain enough of an advantage in the mountains to haul back the losses he gave up to Anquetil against the clock. It was said that Anquetil was a rider who couldn't drop anyone in the mountains, but also a rider no one else could drop. Poulidor was in excellent physical shape and superb form going into the 1964 Tour de France, having won the 1964 Vuelta a España and the Critérium National. He had also was second in the Milan–San Remo and Dauphiné Libéré and fourth in the Paris–Nice. However, the 1964 Tour de France final general classification read as follows:

1. Jacques Anquetil (St Raphaël-Gitane): 127 hrs 9 mins 44 secs
2. Raymond Poulidor (Mercier-BP) at 55 secs.

In total, Poulidor took part in 14 Tours de France and won seven stages, but surprisingly he never wore the yellow jersey and had a best-place finish of second on three occasions (1964, 1965 and 1974).

✵ FIVE CONSECUTIVE STAGE WINS ✵

René Pottier (France) won five consecutive stages (Stages 2–6) in the 1906 Tour de France on his way to clinching the overall yellow jersey. In January 1907, René Pottier hanged himself in the clubhouse of his Peugeot team after learning that his wife was having an affair while he was riding the 1906 Tour de France.

❋ COLOMBIA'S FIRST ❋

When Luis Herrera crossed the line at l'Alpe d'Huez on Stage 17 of the 1984 Tour de France, he became the first Colombian in the history of the Tour to win a stage. He was also the first amateur stage winner in Tour history. After his victory the president of Colombia called Herrera to congratulate him and let him know that the entire country had watched his exploits late into the night (France is seven hours ahead of Colombia).

❋ RIDER THROWS GEAR INTO RAVINE ❋

Prior to Stage 10 of the 1957 Tour de France, Federico Bahamontes (Spain) threw his shoes down a ravine and quit the race. The previous year he had thrown his bike down a ravine before quitting the Tour.

❋ TOUR SPOKESMEN (26) ❋

"You'd see him there, with that smile on his face and you couldn't tell whether he was tired, faking it or laughing at you."
Claudio Chiappucci on Miguel Indurain

❋ COMICAL MERCKX ❋

Eddy Merckx makes a cameo appearance as a "fast runner" in the French cartoon book *Asterix in Belgium*.

❋ TAKING A DIP ❋

Stage 15 of the 1950 Tour de France took the riders from Toulon to Menton along the southern coast of France. During the stage, which was raced on a blistering hot day, the peloton was feeling unmotivated as it rode by the Mediterranean Sea. To the amazement and anger of Tour boss Jacques Goddet, about half of the riders got off their bikes and took a cooling dip in the sea still wearing their cycling attire.

❋ TOUR DEATHS (2) ❋

In 1935, Francisco Cepeda (Spain) died after plunging down a ravine on the Col du Galiber.

❋ TOUR WINNER REFUSES TO BE IN YELLOW ❋

The 1978 Tour de France started in Leiden, Holland and the opening prologue witnessed a torrential rainstorm. Dutch riders dominated the stage and the conditions by claiming the top four places of the time trial: Jan Raas, Gerrie Knetemann, Joop Zoetemelk and Hennie Kuiper. All but Zoetemelk rode for the TI-Raleigh team. However, as a result of the appalling weather conditions the team directors, except TI-Raleigh's Peter Post, held a meeting and decided to petition the Tour organisers to have the results of the prologue discarded towards the General Classification. Amazingly, the Tour organisers agreed to the directors' request and although the prologue results stood, they would not be used in calculating the overall standings. To add insult to injury Raas, winner of the prologue, was denied the honour of wearing the yellow jersey for the start of Stage 1. When the Tour organisers asked Bernard Thévenet, winner of the 1977 Tour, to wear the *maillot jaune* for that first stage, the Frenchman declined the privilege out of respect for Raas's prologue victory.

❋ TOUR WINNER FOUND DEAD ❋

On 3 June 1927, Ottavio Bottecchia, winner of the Tour de France in 1924 and 1925, was found murdered in the Italian countryside. His skull and several bones in his body had been broken. Bottecchia, the first Italian to win the overall yellow jersey, had been out riding his bike, which was found a short distance from where his body lay. At the time many believed that Bottecchia, an outspoken socialist and popular personality in his homeland, was murdered because he was proving to be an embarrassment to the Fascist government led by Benito Mussolini.

❋ OVER TO YOU ❋

Following his fifth Tour de France win in 1985, Bernard Hinault is reported to have said to his La Vie Claire teammate, Greg LeMond, who gave up his own chance of overall victory in the 1985 Tour de France: "In '86 the Tour will be for you. I'll be there to help you." That 1985 Tour saw not only the entry of American LeMond with his ace climbing friend and compatriot Andy Hampsten and Canadian Steve Bauer, but also the entry of the first American team, 7 Eleven-Hoonved.

❋ GAUL WINS AS RACE OFFICIAL DIES ❋

Going into the penultimate stage (23) of the 1958 Tour de France, a 74-kilometre individual time trial, Charly Gaul (Holland/Luxembourg) lay third in the GC at 1 minute 7 seconds behind Vito Favero (Italy). Gaul had already won the previous two time trials and in Stage 23 he beat both Favero and the second-placed rider in the general classification, Raphaël Géminiani (France Centre-Midi), by over 3 minutes to claim the yellow jersey. All Gaul had to do was ride safely into Paris to win the Tour, which he did in a total time of 116 hours 59 minutes 5 seconds, with Vito Favero second at 3 minutes 10 seconds. However, Gaul's victory was marred by a terrible accident. When the sprinters raced to the finish line inside the Parc de Princes velodrome, André Darrigade crashed into Constans Wouters, the manager of the velodrome, who had inadvertently stepped on to the track. Darrigade got back on his bike and finished the stage, after which he received several stitches; however Wouters died from his injuries 11 days later.

❋ SEVEN TAKES OUT 77 ❋

The weather was so bad during the 1909 Tour de France that 77 riders had already abandoned the race after seven stages. It is generally believed that the 1909 Tour de France was raced in the coldest weather ever.

❋ FROM *L'AUTO* TO *L'EQUIPE* ❋

When Paris was liberated in 1944, the authorities put *L'Auto* out of business because it had continued to publish during the German occupation of France. However, Jacques Goddet simply moved offices across the street and founded *L'Equipe* in 1946. As *L'Auto* no longer existed, ownership of the Tour de France was up for grabs so the French Cycling Federation decided to have a race shoot-out between those organisations applying to take over the running of the Tour. The organisation which hosted the most popular cycle race would win the right to take control of organising the Tour. *Sports*, the rival paper to Goddet's *L'Equipe*, joined up with another Parisian paper, *Miroir Sprint*, and held a five-day "Ronde de France" hoping to win the Federation's approval. Goddet's test race, the Monaco–Paris or "La Course du Tour de France" also had five stages. *L'Equipe* received help from another publication, *Le Parisien Libéré*, as well as the owners of the Parc des Princes velodrome. Goddet's race was a success and he won the right to organise the Tour de France.

❋ GREAT CLIMBS (6) – COL DU GALIBIER ❋

The Col du Galibier is one of the most fearsome of all the *hors catégorie* climbs on the Tour de France, rising 2,645m into the Alps. Usually, the man who leads the field over the Galibier will earn the Souvenir Henri Desgrange, a medal (and €5,000) awarded to the man who leads over the highest overall point of each Tour. Almost every great mountain climber has led over the Galibier, which is rarely a stage finish, but none more than twice. And there is one notable exception from the roll of honour: six-time King of the Mountains Richard Virenque.

Location: The département of Savoie and region of Dauphiné Alps in SE France.

Nearest town: Valloire.

Height: 2,645m, though it was 2,556 until a new road was built in 1978.

Gradient: From the Col du Lautaret in the south, the 8.5 climb has an average gradient of 6.9 percent, but 12.1 percent at the summit. From the north, from Valloire, the climb is 18.1km at an average of 6.9 percent, but 10.1 at the summit.

Characteristics: The Col du Galibier has a memorial to Henri Desgrange, the Founder of the Tour, and when the Tour passes by, a wreath is always laid by the riders in his honour. There is a road tunnel near the summit, with traffic flow controlled by a set of lights, one of the highest traffic signals in Europe.

Tour visits: 54, including two stages in 2011 to mark the Galibier's Tour centenary (the highest stage finish in Tour history). A 1996 visit was cancelled because of bad weather.

Multiple winners: 2: Honoré Barthelemy (1919, 1921), Henri Pélissier (1914, 1923), Fédérico Ezquerra (1934, 1936), Charly Gaul (1955, 1959), Federico Bahamontes (1954, 1964), Julio Jiminez (1966, 1967), Andy Schleck (2011, both stages).

Conquerors of the peak: Emile Georget (1911), Eugène Christophe (1912), Marcel Buysse (1913), Firmin Lambot (1920), Emile Masson (1922), Lucien Buysse (1925), Omer Huyse (1926), Antonin Magne

(1927), August Verdyck (1928), Gaston Rebry (1929), Pierre Magne (1930), Jef Demuysere (1931), Francesco Camusso (1932), Vicente Trueba (1933), Gaby Ruozzi (1935), Gino Bartali (1937), Mario Vicini (1938), Dante Gianello (1939), Fermo Camellini (1947), Lucien Teisseire (1948), Fausto Coppi (1952), Marcel Janssens (1957), Eddy Merckx (1969), Joop Zoetemelk (1972), Luis Ocana (1973), Vicente Lopez-Carril (1974), Lucien Van Impe (1979), Johan De Muynck (1980), Jean-François Rodriguez (1984), Luis Herrera (1986), Pedro Muñoz (1987), Gert-Jan Theunise (1989), Franco Chioccioli (1992), Toni Rominger (1993), Marco Pantani (1998), Pascal Herve (2000), Santiago Botero (2002), Stefano Garzelli (2003), Alexandre Vinokourov (2005), Rémy Di Gregorio (2008).

Did You Know That?
Col du Galibier debuted in the 1911 Tour and was such a challenge that only three men rode all the way to the summit: Emile Georget, Paul Duboc and Gustave Garrigou.

❋ TOUR SPOKESMEN (27) ❋

"I've tried to win with style."
Richard Virenque, multiple King of the Mountains winner

❋ A QUICK RELEASE ❋

In 1937, Tullio Campagnolo invented the quick release wheel. Prior to Campagnolo's idea for changing gears a rider had to dismount, loosen the wing nuts and either move the chain to the other rear sprocket or flip the wheel around to get access to the other two cogs.

❋ THE DEFIANT IRISHMAN ❋

In the 1987 Giro d'Italia Stephen Roche rode alongside Roberto Visentini on the Italian "Carrera" team. During a time trial the Irishman had lost the leader's jersey to Visentini, but when the race entered the mountains Roche sped past Visentini who was unable to keep up with the leaders. Roche's team director told him to wait for his struggling leader but the plucky Irish rider refused and raced up the mountain to retake the leader's pink jersey. Visentini came in many minutes after Roche and was completely out of contention for the overall victory. He later abandoned the race, while Roche rode to victory before going on to claim the yellow jersey in Paris that July.

✻ TOUR TURNED UPSIDE DOWN ✻

Going into Stage 10 of the 1923 Tour de France, Henri Pélissier (Automoto) lay in third place in the GC at 22 minutes 8 seconds to his teammate, Ottavio Bottecchia. Pélissier, assisted by his brother Francis (Automoto), rode majestically on Stage 10 from Nice to Briançon, which took in climbs up the Allos, the Vars and the massive Izoard. Pélissier's Stage 10 victory turned the GC upside down as he was now in yellow followed by Jean Alavoine at 11 minutes 25 seconds. Ottavio Bottecchia came in 12th in Stage 10 at 41 minutes 8 seconds behind his teammate, and was now third in the GC at 13 minutes 16 seconds. Henri Pélissier went on to claim overall victory in Paris.

✻ PRETTY IN WHITE ✻

France has dominated the *maillot blanc* (the white jersey awarded to the best young rider in the Tour de France) since it was first awarded in the 1975 Tour. France has won six *maillots blancs* with their last win, by Pierre Rolland (Team Europcar), coming in 2011. Italy, Netherlands and Spain have all had five winners while Tejay van Garderen (BMC Racing Team) became the third American to win the white jersey in 2012 after Greg LeMond (Renault) in 1984 and Andrew Hampsten (La Vie Claire) in 1996.

✻ AN AMAZING VICTORY ✻

Roger Lapébie (France) won the 1937 Tour de France. Lapébie and Henri Desgrange had fought from Lapébie's very first Tour until Desgrange's retirement as race organiser in 1936, and sometimes the arguments kept Lapébie off the French team. Indeed in 1935 he rode as an *individuel*, but abandoned the race after the twelfth stage, resulting in another heated argument with Desgrange. Lapébie, who had finished third in the 1934 Tour, sat out the 1936 edition of the race. However when Jacques Goddet became the new Tour manager for 1937, Lapébie was back on his bike for France, who wanted to prevent the Belgians from winning their third consecutive Tour de France. What is so remarkable about Lapébie's victory in the 1937 Tour de France is that prior to the race there were doubts about his form; he had undergone back surgery for a lumbar hernia after riding the motor-paced 500-kilometre Bordeaux–Paris race. Amazingly the Bordeaux–Paris race started on 30 May 1937 while the Tour started on 30 June 1937.

✳ PRIZE MONEY DOUBLED ✳

In 1952 the Tour organisers feared that Fausto Coppi's runaway victory would result in a loss of interest in the Tour de France among the general public. Their reaction was to double the prize money for finishing second and third, thereby encouraging the riders to race more aggressively.

✳ TOUR SPOKESMEN (28) ✳

"This is a hard Tour and hard work wins it. Vive le Tour."
Lance Armstrong

✳ VIRENQUE RETURNS ✳

After his Festina Team was kicked out of the 1998 Tour, Richard Virenque (Team Polti) ended his Tour exile in 2000 by winning a dramatic stage into Morzine, his first stage victory since 1997. The French cyclist failed, however, to win his sixth King of the Mountains polka dot jersey.

✳ THE ARGENTINE ✳

Lucien Petit-Breton was the winner of the 1907 Tour de France (47 points to Gustave Garrigou's 66), but this was not his real name. He was actually named Lucien Mazan and sometimes referred to as "The Argentine" because his father had emigrated to Buenos Aires. His father did not want his son to race bicycles, so the young Mazan took a pseudonym in order to keep his occupation secret from the family.

✳ FORK IN THE ROAD ✳

On the Col du Galibier during Stage 11 of the 1922 Tour de France, Eugène Christophe broke his forks for an unbelievable third time. The unlucky French rider had also suffered broken forks at crucial moments during the 1913 and 1919 Tours. Once again he had to walk his bike down a mountain and make his own repairs.

✳ DOUBLE YELLOW ✳

In 1957, André Darrigade won the first stage and the year's first yellow jersey for the second successive year.

❊ GREEN JERSEY WINNERS ❊

Year	Winner	Country
1953	Fritz Schär	Switzerland
1954	Ferdi Kübler	Switzerland
1955	Stan Ockers	Belgium
1956	Stan Ockers	Belgium
1957	Jean Forestier	France
1958	Jean Graczyk	France
1959	André Darrigade	France
1960	Jean Graczyk	France
1961	André Darrigade	France
1962	Rudi Altig	Germany
1963	Rik Van Looy	Belgium
1964	Jan Janssen	Netherlands
1965	Jan Janssen	Netherlands
1966	Willy Planckaert	Belgium
1967	Jan Janssen	Netherlands
1968	France Bitossi	Italy
1969	Eddy Merckx	Belgium
1970	Walter Godefroot	Belgium
1971	Eddy Merckx	Belgium
1972	Eddy Merckx	Belgium
1973	Herman Van Springel	Belgium
1974	Patrick Sercu	Belgium
1975	Rik Van Linden	Belgium
1976	Freddy Maertens	Belgium
1977	Jacques Esclassan	France
1978	Freddy Maertens	Belgium
1979	Bernard Hinault	France
1980	Rudy Pevenage	Belgium
1981	Freddy Maertens	Belgium
1982	Sean Kelly	Ireland
1983	Sean Kelly	Ireland
1984	Frank Hoste	Belgium
1985	Sean Kelly	Ireland
1986	Eric Vanderaerden	Belgium
1987	Jean-Paul van Poppel	Netherlands
1988	Eddy Plankaert	Belgium
1989	Sean Kelly	Ireland
1990	Olaf Ludwig	Germany
1991	Djamolidine Abdoujaparov	Uzbekistan
1992	Laurent Jalabert	France

1993	Djamolidine Abdoujaparov	Uzbekistan
1994	Djamolidine Abdoujaparov	Uzbekistan
1995	Laurent Jalabert	France
1996	Erik Zabel	Germany
1997	Erik Zabel	Germany
1998	Erik Zabel	Germany
1999	Erik Zabel	Germany
2000	Erik Zabel	Germany
2001	Erik Zabel	Germany
2002	Robbie McEwen	Australia
2003	Baden Cooke	Australia
2004	Robbie McEwen	Australia
2005	Thor Hushovd	Norway
2006	Robbie McEwen	Australia
2007	Tom Boonen	Belgium
2008	Óscar Freire	Spain
2009	Thor Hushovd	Norway
2010	Alessandro Petacchi	Italy
2011	Mark Cavendish	Great Britain
2012	Peter Sagan	Slovakia

❋ SWISS MASTER ❋

On his way to winning the 1951 Tour de France at his first attempt, the Swiss rider Hugo Koblet won five stages. Six years after he retired from cycling, Koblet died in a car crash aged just 39. Some witnesses who saw the crash believe Koblet committed suicide as they watched him drive his white Alfa Romeo straight into a tree without any apparent attempt by him to avert the crash. In a somewhat bizarre twist of fate, the doctor who was first at the scene and who later confirmed Koblet's death was named Kübler, the same surname as Koblet's great Swiss rival, Ferdy Kübler.

❋ TEAM ASTANA TAKE A BREAK ❋

On 31 July 2007 the Swiss-based Astana team, financially backed by the Kazakhstan government, announced that they had suspended all activities for one month following the dismissal of their team leader Alexandre Vinokourov during the 2007 Tour de France for failing a blood doping test after a stage win on 14 July 2007. A team statement read: "Following recent events, we have decided to stop our activities until the end of August. This period of time will be the opportunity for deep questioning."

❊ A FIGHT TO THE LINE ❊

Stage 9 of the 1970 Tour de France took the race from Saarluis in Germany to Mulhouse, France and produced a dramatic day's racing. On the final ascent of the day, up the Grand Ballon, Joaquim Agostinho and Mogens Frey (both members of the Frimatic team) broke away. When it came down to the sprint Agostinho was of the opinion that his Danish teammate wouldn't contest it given that the Portuguese rider had done much of the work at the front, so he stepped on the gas. However, to the amazement and anger of Agostinho, Frey started to come around him and raced him to the line. A somewhat furious Agostinho rode his bike to the side of the road, forcing his teammate to take the long way around, but the young Dane kept coming, resulting in Agostinho putting his hands out to block him before grabbing Frey's jersey to cross the line first. Following his win, the band played the Portuguese national anthem to celebrate Agostinho's victory while the rider did a victory lap. However, the race jury awarded the stage to Frey and relegated Agostinho to second place. Their Frimatic team boss was so furious with them that he forced them to share the same hotel room that night.

❊ CADETS AND BLEUETS ❊

Up to and including 1937, a rider could enter the Tour de France as an *individuel* and compete at his own expense, but in 1938 the *individuel* classification was abolished. In 1937, the runner-up, Mario Vicini, was an *individuel*. However, rather than ban some 20 very good French riders from the Tour just because they were not selected for the national team, two new categories were introduced: Cadets and Bleuets.

❊ THE UNLUCKY RIDER ❊

During the penultimate stage of the 1919 Tour de France, Stage 14 from Metz to Dunkirk, disaster once again befell Eugène Christophe. In the suburbs of Valenciennes, Christophe broke his fork just as he had done in 1913. Once again he had to walk his bike with its broken fork to a forge and repair it himself. At the time he was in yellow at 28 minutes 5 seconds from Firmin Lambot. He lost over 70 minutes fixing his bike, and lost a total time of 2 hours 28 minutes. It was the end of his hopes of staying in yellow all the way to Paris. Firmin Lambot won the 1919 Tour de France, while Christophe was third.

❋ FRANCE'S STAGE KING ❋

André Leducq (France) won the Tour de France in 1930 and 1932 and held the record for the most number of stage victories, 25, until Eddy Merckx surpassed it with a total of 34.

❋ A GROWING PELOTON ❋

In 1903, the inaugural Tour de France comprised a total of 60 riders. Over the Tour's lengthy history the peloton has increased quite considerably:

1903: 60
1911: 80
1920: 113
1930: 100
1939: 79
1950: 116
1960: 128
1970: 150
1975: 140
2005: 189
2009: 180

❋ HISTORY REPEATS ITSELF ❋

Stage 2 of the 1924 Tour de France was 371 kilometres long and since it needed over 14 hours to complete, the stage was started before sunrise. When the riders set off the weather was cool, so Henri Pélissier wore a couple of jerseys. As the day warmed up Pélissier took off his outer layer and threw it away. Eberado Pavesi, manager of the Legnano team, witnessed this infraction of Rule 48 and reported the matter to Desgrange. Rule 48 stipulated that a rider must finish the stage with everything he had at the start and as a result Pélissier was penalised. Four years earlier Pélissier quit the Tour after another of his infamous run-ins with Desgrange, but this time he accepted the penalty and remained in the race.

❋ TOUR SPOKESMEN (29) ❋

"Why not just give the jersey to Contador tomorrow and say, 'Here you are – instead of racing to Paris we'll go on holiday'?"
Stephen Roche, on Alberto Contador's rivals' failure to challenge him in the 2009 race

✤ TOUR LEGENDS (7) – GREG LeMOND ✤

Greg LeMond was born on 26 June 1961 in Lakewood, California, USA. At the Junior World Championships in 1979 he won gold, silver and bronze medals with the Renault-Elf-Gitane racing team. After turning professional in 1981, LeMond finished second in the 1982 World Cycling Championships. A year later, he won the Dauphiné Libéré in the spring and became the first American to win the famous rainbow jersey as World Road Race Cycling champion. Greg now turned his attention to the sport's Grand Tours.

In 1984, he rode in his maiden Tour de France and stood on the podium in Paris after finishing third overall. Bernard Hinault won the prologue of the 1984 Tour, with LeMond ninth, just 12 seconds behind the master time triallist. A teammate of the eventual Tour winner, Laurent Fignon, LeMond's third-place finish was good enough to earn him the prestigious white jersey as the Tour's best young rider.

For 1985, Greg joined the La Vie Claire team, under *directeur sportif* Paul Koechli. LeMond was under strict instructions from Koechli to ride in support of team-leader Bernard Hinault. However, towards the end of that Tour, Hinault began to suffer, but LeMond was ordered not to attack the yellow jersey. Instead of claiming the yellow jersey, LeMond had to settle for second place overall, behind Hinault, who thus claimed a record-equalling five Tour victories. In the 1986 Tour, however, Hinault and LeMond were equal leaders of the La Vie Claire team and LeMond seized the moment by winning the overall classification, thereby becoming the first American to wear the yellow jersey in Paris.

On 20 April 1987, out on a turkey hunt, LeMond was accidentally shot by his brother-in-law. Greg suffered injuries serious enough to force him to miss the Tour in both 1987 and 1988. He returned for the 1989 Tour and, going into the final-stage time trial, trailed Fignon by 50 seconds. A miraculous effort in the time trial saw LeMond take 58 seconds out of the Frenchman to win the Tour by the slenderest margin of victory ever, a mere eight seconds. Seven weeks later, he won his second rainbow jersey.

LeMond won his third overall yellow jersey in 1990 and is one of only seven riders who have three or more Tour victories to their name. Amazingly, he failed to win a single stage in the 1990 Tour. His 1992 Tour DuPont victory proved to be his last win as a professional and – after being diagnosed with a heart condition – he retired from professional cycling.

Did You Know That?
LeMond was named *Sports Illustrated* magazine's 1989 Sportsman of the Year, the first cyclist ever to receive the prestigious award.

❋ TOUR SPOKESMEN (30) ❋

"Champagne does taste a wee bit better after you have crossed the line on the Champs-Elysées in yellow."
Cadel Evans, winner of the 2011 Tour de France

❋ ME AND EDDY CLEANED UP ❋

Despite winning the Tour de France and the Giro d'Italia five times, Eddy Merckx never won the classic Paris–Tours race during his outstanding career. When the Belgian cyclist Noel Van Tyghem won the classic in 1972, he was quoted as saying: "Together with Merckx, I won all classics that can be won. I won Paris–Tours, Merckx won all the rest."

❋ THE LAND OF THE RISING SUN ❋

The 2009 Tour de France, the 96th edition of the famous race, saw two Japanese riders join the pack: Fumiyuki Beppu (Skil-Shimano), who finished in 112th place, and Yukiya Arashiro (BBox Bouygues Telecom), who came home in 129th place. The first Japanese rider to ride in the Tour was Kisso Kawamuro who rode in the 1926 and 1927 races, failing both times in his attempt to reach Paris. In 1996 Daisuke Imanaka rode in the Tour for the Polti team, but like Kawamuro he never saw the finish line in Paris.

❋ RIDER PAID TO STAY AWAY ❋

Alfredo Binda abandoned the 1930 Tour de France after Stage 9 of the race which was the riders' second day in the Pyrenees. Binda won the Giro d'Italia in 1925, 1927, 1928 and 1929 and in 1930 the organisers of the Giro actually paid him the same amount of money that the 1930 Giro winner would receive just to stay away from the race. The organisers felt that yet another Binda domination of Italy's most prestigious race would make it uninteresting for the spectators. Upon learning this news Desgrange approached Binda and asked him to ride in the 1930 Tour de France. Binda wanted payment from Desgrange to race and therefore a secret contract was agreed upon whose existence Binda revealed only in 1980, six years before his death.

✻ COMETH THE HOUR, COMETH THE CHRONO ✻

In 1934 Henri Desgrange tinkered with the Tour de France format yet again and introduced the first individual time trial (or *chrono*) as the second part of a two-stage day. The previous two Tours resulted in very close finishes, and had it not been for the generous 4-minute time bonuses for stage wins the final standings for the overall general classifications would have looked slightly different. Consequently a 90-kilometre time trial with only three stages remaining in the 1934 Tour could prove decisive. On Friday 27 July 1934, Antonin Magne (France) made history by winning the Tour's first individual time trial and went on to claim overall victory on the podium in Paris, his second Tour de France win. Time trials are now known as *contre-la-montre* (against the clock).

✻ LUXEMBOURG TOUR WINNERS ✻

1	2 wins	Nicolas Frantz (1927, 1928)
2	1 win	François Faber (1909)
=	1 win	Charly Gaul (1958)
=	1 win	Andy Schleck (2010)

✻ FIRST TOUR, FIRST DAY IN YELLOW ✻

The opening Prologue of the 1977 Tour de France was a 5-kilometre time trial in Fleurence, just north of the Pyrenees. Dietrich Thurau won it, beating his TI-Raleigh teammate Gerrie Knetemann by 4 seconds and Eddy Merckx by 8 seconds. It was Thurau's first day in his first Tour and the German rider wore the yellow jersey proudly. Thurau turned professional in 1974 and won five major races including his national Championship.

✻ THE CREAM ALWAYS RISES TO THE TOP ✻

In 2008, Andy Schleck (Team CSC Saxo Bank) won the *maillot blanc* which is awarded to the best young rider who finishes a Tour de France. He finished 12th overall in the 2008 Tour to Spain's Carlos Sastre (Rabobank). In the 2009 Tour de France Schleck (Team Saxo Bank) retained his *maillot blanc* and finished runner-up in the Tour to Alberto Contador (Astana). Following the post-Tour disqualification of Contador from the 2010 event, Schleck became only the fourth rider to win both the *maillot blanc* and the coveted *maillot jaune* in the same year.

❋ TAPEWORM SCARE ❋

Jacques Anquetil's participation in the 1963 Tour de France was in doubt as he had been infected with a tapeworm and his doctors advised against competing in the race. However, Anquetil went against his doctors' orders and won his fourth *maillot jaune*, a Tour record number of wins at the time.

❋ TOUR SPOKESMEN (31) ❋

"I need to get to the line first and that's about all I think about."
Mark Cavendish, winner of the Tour de France green jersey

❋ ALMOST A CLEAN SWEEP OF JERSEYS ❋

In the 1986 Tour de France one team dominated, La Vie Claire. Greg LeMond won the *maillot jaune* while his teammate and winner of the 1985 Tour de France, Bernard Hinault, was second. Hinault won the polka dot jersey awarded to the King of the Mountains, Andrew Hampsten won the Best Young Rider award, the *maillot blanc*, LeMond also claimed the combination award, and La Vie Claire won the team award.

❋ PELOTON ENTERS ENGLAND ❋

In 1974, the Tour de France held a stage in England for the first time in the 71-year history of the race. Stage 2 was held in Plymouth with the entire Tour being ferried over to race on an as yet unopened highway. British Immigration, however, held the riders up for several hours on their way back to France. The Tour organisers were unimpressed with British hospitality and it would be a further 10 years before the Tour crossed the English Channel again.

❋ GINO'S LAST ❋

With an 11th-place finish in the 1953 Tour de France, Gino Bartali ended his last Tour. He rode the Tour eight times, starting in 1937, and finished six of them. The Italian legend won two Tours (1938 and 1948) and in both races he claimed the climber's prize (the King of the Mountain's jersey was not introduced until 1975). Bartali retired from professional racing a year later and during his illustrious career, he lost and gave away most of his money but always retained his famous religious piety. Gino Bartali passed away in 2000.

❋ GREAT CLIMBS (7) – COL DU LAUTARET ❋

The Col du Lautaret is recognised as one of the giants of the Tour, but it has not been a regular feature of the Tour for almost half a century. It appeared in 24 out of 45 Tours 1911–65, but since then, only twice each in the 1970s and 2000s. As a climb it is not considered very taxing and is no longer considered an *hors cat´gorie* challenge. In fact, in the 2006 Tour, it was only a category 2 climb, coming between *hors catégorie* climbs of the Col d'Izoard (2,380m) and l'Alpe d'Huez (1,850m).

Location: The département of Hautes-Alpes, the ridge forming the boundary between the Rhône-Alpes and Provence-Alpes-Côte d'Azur regions in France.

Nearest town: Briançon.

Height: 2,058m.

Gradient: From Briançon the gradient to the summit is only 3.1 percent; it rises 853m over 27.75km. In 2006, from the Col d'Izoard, the gradient was 4.4 percent.

Characteristics: The Col du Lautaret was formed by a glacier. Although it has 2,058m elevation, it is actually one of the lower passes in the High Alps. Route Nationale 91 (from Grenoble to Briançon) climbs Lautaret.

Tour visits: 28.

Multiple winners: Honoré Barthélémy (1919 and 1921).

Conquerors of the peak: Emile Georget (1911), Eugène Christophe (1912), Marcel Buysse (1913), Henri Pélissier (1914), Honoré Barthelemy (1919, 1921), Antonin Magne (1928), Gaston Rebry (1929), Fernand Robache (1930), Maurice de Waele (1931), Vicente Trueba (1933), René Vietto (1934), Gaby Ruozzi (1935), Fédérico Ezquerra (1936), Gino Bartali (1937), Fermo Camellini (1947), Louison Bobet (1948), Jean-Apo Lazarides (1950), Gino Sciardis (1951), Jean le Guilly (1953), Piet Van Est (1958), Jean Graczyk (1960), Juan Campillo (1962), Francisco Gabica (1965), Joaquim Agostinho (1972), Luciano Conati (1976), Danilo di Luca (2003), David de la Fuente (2006).

Did You Know That?
Twenty-year-old René Vietto earned Tour de France legend status when he cycled back down to the mountain to help his team-leader Antonin Magne, who had crashed. Magne won the Tour, while Vietto's reward was the King of the Mountains title.

❋ WHO PUT THAT COW THERE? ❋

On Stage 2 of the 1912 Tour de France, a 388-kilometre ride from Dunkirk to Longwy, Lucien Petit-Breton (Tour winner in 1907 and 1908) crashed out of the race after hitting a cow.

❋ THE KING IS BORN ❋

In 1933 Henri Desgrange decided that points would be accumulated in a competition for the first rider over each mountain, and the tougher the climb, the more points would be awarded. This was the birth of the "King of the Mountains" competition. The King of the Mountains competition's first sponsor was Martini & Rossi of vermouth fame. Although the prestigious competition actually began in 1933, the famous polka dot jersey (*maillot à pois*), awarded to the best climber in the Tour, was not introduced until 1975. The Belgian rider, Lucien Van Impe, was the first to wear the *maillot à pois*.

❋ GOING DUTCH ❋

Like the 1954 Tour, the 1973 Tour de France started in Holland, only this time from the town of Scheveningen. Joop Zoetemelk, the reigning Dutch road champion, had the privilege of winning the first stage (a 7.1-kilometre prologue) in his home country and with it the *maillot jaune*, much to the joy of the Dutch spectators.

❋ THE EUROPEAN TOUR DE FRANCE ❋

The 1992 Tour de France embraced the signing of the Maastricht Treaty by hosting stages in Spain, France, Germany, Holland, Belgium, Italy and Luxembourg. The race began with a prologue in San Sebastian, Spain, and was won by the home favourite and reigning champion, Miguel Indurain. A new face to the Tour, Switzerland's Alex Zülle riding for the Spanish ONCE team, finished just two seconds behind Big Mig. The following day Zülle was in yellow after he managed to snatch an intermediate time bonus.

❋ MERCKX VICTORY SALUTE COSTS HIM WIN ❋

Stage 15 of the 1972 Tour de France was a short 28-kilometre ride up Mount Revard. Eddy Merckx and Cyrille Guimard raced one another to the finish line and Merckx was so sure he would cross the line first that he took one hand off the handlebars to signal victory. However Guimard's reflexes and timing were excellent, and noticing Merckx ease up slightly the young French rider threw his bike across the line to claim the stage win.

❋ FRENCH TOUR DE FORCE IS SHOCKED ❋

The French team entered for the 1959 Tour de France was one of the strongest the nation ever assembled. The 12-man team contained riders such as Louison Bobet (winner of the Tour in 1953, 1954 and 1955) who was looking to become the first rider to win four Tours, Jacques Anquetil (Tour winner in 1957), Raphaël Géminiani (third in 1958), Robert Cazala; André Darrigade (the greatest sprinter of his generation), René Privat; and Roger Rivière (two-times World Professional Pursuit Champion and World Hour Record holder). However, in the end Federico Bahamontes (Spain) won the Tour in a time of 123 hours 46 minutes 45 seconds, while the highest-placed French rider was not even a member of the national "Tour de Force" team. Henry Anglade, of the France Centre-Midi team, finished as runner-up at 4 minutes 1 second.

❋ TOUR SPOKESMEN (32) ❋

"I thought it was the honourable thing to do. Nobody wants to benefit from someone else's misfortune."
Bradley Wiggins, who allowed Cadel Evans to close up on Stage 14 of 2012 Tour de France after tacks on the road caused a flat tyre

❋ BARTALI–COPPI REUNION ❋

After refusing to ride for the Italian national team in the 1948 Tour de France, Fausto Coppi returned to the Tour in 1949 to ride alongside his fellow countryman and 1948 Tour winner, Gino Bartali. It was now down to the Italian team manager Alfredo Binda to get the best out of the two without the pair fighting one another. However, 1949 belonged solely to Coppi and even before he arrived in France for the start of the 1949 Tour, which he won, he had already won the 1949 Giro d'Italia (his third) with a magnificent display of racing, beating Bartali by 23 minutes 47 seconds.

❋ FESTINA TEAM EXPELLED FROM TOUR ❋

Prior to the start of the 1998 Tour de France the Festina team was generally considered to be the world's top professional cycling team. However, during the 1998 Tour the entire Festina team was expelled from the race following the discovery two weeks earlier of over 400 phials of performance-enhancing drugs in a Festina team car driven by masseur Willy Voet. The riders included four-times King of the Mountains winner Richard Virenque and the World Road Race Champion Laurent Brochard. Tour de France officials took the unprecedented step of expelling the Festina team after their team director Bruno Roussel admitted his riders were on a programme of doping. All nine riders and team officials were questioned by the police in Lyon, home of the Festina team.

❋ EDDY THE GREATEST ❋

In 2000 the Belgian magazine *Knack* proclaimed Eddy Merckx as "The Belgian of the Century" and in 2004 another magazine, *Humo*, called him "The Greatest Ever Belgian".

❋ LEND ME A WHEEL ❋

Up to and including the 1922 Tour de France a rider had to carry out his own repairs, but in 1923 Henri Desgrange changed the rules so that riders were now permitted to swap parts, so that a rider wouldn't have to repair his bike while he was leading a stage. However, every rider still had to finish each stage with everything he had at the start.

❋ BIG MIG'S UNIQUE DOUBLE ❋

Miguel Indurain (Banesto) went into the 1993 Tour de France after winning the Giro d'Italia just as he had done in 1992 and then became the first rider ever to win the two major races in back-to-back years.

❋ THE RISE OF PROFESSIONALISM ❋

Every rider who finished in the top 10 at the end of the 1953 Tour de France had turned professional after the end of the Second World War. The average speed set a new Tour record, previously clocked at 31.9 kph, but now up to 34.6 kph.

❋ GREAT TOURS DE FRANCE (7): 1969 ❋

There were seven different overall prizes on offer at the 1969 Tour de France and Faema's Eddy Merckx collared six of them. The only title to elude the man nicknamed "The Cannibal" was the intermediate sprints title. Merckx also came close to the unusual feat of leading from the prologue, but he lost out narrowly to Rudi Altig. From Stage 9, the 111km (69 miles) from Thanon-les-Bains to Chamonix, Merckx held the yellow (overall), polka dot (mountains), green (points – sprint) and white (combination) jerseys. Faema – his team – wrested the team jersey from KAS on Stage 17, and Merckx also won the Combativity award. In almost any other year, Roger Pingeon would have made the headlines, coming second in the overall and mountains classification and fourth in the points, but he finished almost 18 minutes behind Merckx.

Rank	Name	Country	Time
1.	Eddy Merckx	Belgium	116h 16' 02"
2.	Roger Pingeon	France	+17' 54"
3.	Raymond Poulidor	France	+22' 13"
4.	Felice Gimondi	Italy	+29' 24"
5.	Andrés Gandarias	Spain	+33' 04"
6.	Marinus Wagtmans	Netherlands	+33' 57"
7.	Pierfranco Vianelli	Italy	+42' 40"
8.	Joaquim Agostinho	Portugal	+51' 24"
9.	Désiré Letort	France	+51' 41"
10.	Jan Janssen	Netherlands	+52' 56"

Did You Know That?
After two years of riders representing national teams, the 1969 Tour saw the return to commercially sponsored teams, and it has remained that way ever since.

❋ TEAM PROLOGUE INTRODUCED ❋

The 1971 Tour de France witnessed the first-ever team prologue, an 11-kilometre sprint won easily by Eddy Merckx (Molteni) and his squad of Italian-sponsored Belgians. They beat the second-placed Ferretti team by 1 minute 48 seconds and Joop Zoetemelk's Flandrias team by 2 minutes 16 seconds. The times didn't count towards the individual General Classification but the result did put Merckx in yellow to let the peloton know that the Cannibal was hungry.

✻ ELEVEN PUNCTURES ✻

In 1921, Louis Mottiat won the opening stage of the Tour de France for the second successive year. Honoré Barthélémy, who had lost the sight in one of his eyes in the previous year's Tour, finished in second place, coming in 2 minutes 37 seconds behind. However, Barthélémy's chances of winning the stage from Paris to Le Havre were greatly hampered with no fewer than 11 punctures.

✻ RIDING UNDER THE ONE FLAG ✻

In 1967 the Tour reverted to national team format. In order to accommodate all the excellent riders from the major cycling nations, three French teams were entered (the second team was known as "Bleuets" and the third "Coqs") while Spain, Belgium and Italy entered two each, and Britain and Holland one each. The main French team contained 1966 winner Lucien Aimar, Raymond Poulidor and Roger Pingeon (who won the 1967 Tour).

✻ TOUR SPOKESMEN (33) ✻

"Being a mountain specialist is very hard, not that I'd rather be anything else because I don't think that you can become…well, let's say a better human being, without effort. You can beat the problems of life much more easily if you've met hardship."
José Manuel Fuente, former pro cyclist, won four consecutive King of the Mountains

✻ FROM THE LAND DOWN UNDER ✻

In 1928, the Ravat-Wonder-Dunlop team was made up of Australians and New Zealanders with Ernest Bainbridge, Hubert Opperman, Perry Osborne and Harry Watson becoming the first men from their countries to participate in the Tour de France. Prior to the start of the 1928 Tour the team travelled to France to attend a training camp, with tickets paid for by the Dunlop tyre company.

✻ SECOND LUXEMBURGER ✻

In 1927, Nicolas Frantz (Alcyon) claimed the first of two consecutive Tour de France wins in a time of 198 hours 16 minutes 42 seconds. He became the second Luxemburger to win the Tour; François Faber won in 1909.

❋ BIG GUNS RETURN ❋

In 1989 Laurent Fignon, who had practically been out of competitive cycling since his Achilles tendon surgery in 1984, was back to his majestic best. The 1983 and 1984 Tour de France winner entered the 1989 Tour having already won the year's Milan–San Remo and the Giro d'Italia. Fignon also had a very strong team behind him, Super U, which included future Tour winner Bjarne Riis (1996). Meanwhile Greg LeMond (ADR) was also back racing following his recovery from a shooting accident, but he was not as strong as Fignon approaching the 1989 Tour. But in the end LeMond's doggedness and personal drive propelled him to his second overall yellow jersey victory in the 1989 Tour.

❋ TOUR AGONY ❋

Louison Bobet's victory in the 1953 Tour de France, his first of three consecutive victories, was not only a triumph of perseverance but also a show of Bobet's willingness to suffer incredible pain in order to ply his craft. Throughout his career the Frenchman was susceptible to boils and on occasion they would break out all over his body. This awful affliction had already struck Bobet in the 1948 Tour. During the 1953 Giro d'Italia, boils forced Bobet to retire on the last stage. He had them lanced and recovered sufficiently to ride in the 1953 Tour. They reappeared in the Pyrenees during the Tour, and yet again had to be lanced by a doctor.

❋ CROSSING THE TRACKS ❋

In 1935, Romain Maes (Belgium) ended France's hopes of six successive Tour de France victories. He got off to a good start when during Stage 1 he managed to place a train between himself and the peloton. Maes beat the chasing pack up to a level crossing and managed to get across the tracks before the road was closed. As the other riders waited impatiently for the train to pass, Maes was able to finish the stage almost a minute ahead of the peloton.

❋ LAST IN FIRST OUT ❋

The 1948 Tour de France covered 4,922 kilometres in 21 stages, and contained a new rule. Between the third and 18th stages, the last man in the general classification would be eliminated.

❋ THE TOURLESS CHAMPIONS TOUR ❋

When the riders assembled for the beginning of the 1956 Tour de France, there were no previous Tour winners in the line. The only other time this had happened since the inaugural Tour in 1903 was in 1927.

❋ LONG RIFLE AIMED AT ANQUETIL ❋

Having won the first of his five Tour de France overall yellow jerseys in 1957, Jacques Anquetil was so important a rider to the French national team that he could practically pick the team himself. For the 1958 Tour Anquetil did not want both Louison Bobet, a three-times Tour winner (1953, 1954, 1955) and Raphaël Géminiani on "his" team; Bobet and Géminiani were close friends, and Anquetil saw their friendship as a threat to his chances of winning future Tours. The manager of the French team Marcel Bidot gave in to Anquetil's request, and chose Bobet to ride in a supporting role to Anquetil. Géminiani, an outspoken character at the best of times, was furious and let the press know it, claiming that he had been "dismissed without a care", Nicknamed *Le Grand Fusil* ("Top Gun") by Bobet, Géminiani sought revenge by teaming up with the France Centre-Midi regional team. Charly Gaul (Luxembourg) prevented Anquetil, who had to abandon the Tour with two stages remaining, from winning successive yellow jerseys. Anquetil had been forced to quit as he was suffering from pulmonary congestion.

❋ FRENCH DELIGHT IN HOLLAND ❋

The first stage of the 1996 Tour de France was held in Holland, a 206-kilometre ride starting and finishing in Hertogenbosch. Frederic Moncassin (France, GAN), who had never before won a Tour stage, won a dramatic sprint ahead of Jeroen Blijlevens (Netherlands, TVM) and Jan Svorada (Czech Republic, Panaria).

❋ NATIONAL PRIDE SELLS PAPERS ❋

In 1933 Henri Desgrange's national team formula had produced its fourth successive French Tour de France victory when Georges Speicher won the overall yellow jersey. National pride soared and interest in the race was at an all-time high as *L'Auto*'s circulation rose to 854,000, a record, to satisfy the public's thirst for knowledge of the Tour and their national heroes.

✵ ORGANISATIONAL CHANGE ✵

In 1962 Emilion Amaury, owner of the newspaper *Le Parisien Libéré*, became financially involved with the Tour de France. Amaury was the man who had helped persuade the French Cycling Federation to award the organisation of the Tour to Jacques Goddet after the end of the Second World War. In the process Felix Levitan, who had been a writer for *Le Parisien Libéré*, became co-organiser of the Tour. Over the years Goddet assumed total control of the sporting side of the Tour, while Levitan effectively became its financial controller. Goddet and Levitan were not friends, but their relationship lasted for a quarter of a century until Levitan was sacked in 1987.

✵ SWITZERLAND TOUR WINNERS ✵

1	1 win	Ferdinand Kübler (1950)
=	1 win	Hugo Koblet (1951)

✵ A NEW STAR ON THE HORIZON ✵

Eddy Merckx started 1976 by winning Milan–San Remo for a seventh time and also won the Catalonian Week. However, the Belgian five-times Tour de France winner was somewhat overshadowed that year by a young fellow Belgian called Freddy Maertens. While Merckx stayed at home, Maertens, who had turned professional in 1972, was making his maiden Tour appearance. Incredibly he won eight stages in the 1976 Tour to equal the record set by Charles Pélissier in 1930 and Merckx in 1970 and 1974. However, it was yet another Belgian rider, Lucien Van Impe, who won the 1976 Tour de France while Maertens had to settle for the points jersey. During the 1976 season Maertens won 54 races including the World Pro Road Championships and the Belgian Road Championships. He was at his peak in 1976 and 1977 before his career started to fizzle out, but his swansong came in 1981 when against all the odds and many personal battles he won that year's World Championship.

✵ UPHILL STRUGGLE ✵

Stage 8 of the 1973 Tour de France was a truly epic day. The riders faced a 237.5-kilometre slog with climbs over the Madeleine, the Télégraphe, the Galibier and the Izoard, followed by an energy-sapping haul to the finish at Les Orres. Luis Ocaña (BIC team) claimed victory, en route to an overall *maillot jaune* victory.

✳ LeMOND WINS BY 82M OVER 3,257KM ✳

Members of the memoire-du-cyclisme website forum calculated that according to the average speeds at which Greg LeMond (ADR) and Laurent Fignon (Super U) were travelling in the final time trial of the 1989 Tour de France, the 8 seconds by which LeMond won the overall yellow jersey equated to approximately 82 metres – at a little more than 90 yards, that is less than the length of a football pitch – and this after both men had completed 20 stages and 3,257 kilometres of racing.

✳ TOUR SPOKESMEN (34) ✳

"The bike is a terrible thing that drives you to make excessive efforts, inhuman efforts. It takes a racing cyclist to understand what it means to hurt yourself on a bike. Apart from that, everything else about cycling is wonderful: the friendships, the tactics, the ambience, the glory."
Jacques Anquetil, former pro cyclist and Tour de France winner

✳ LEST WE FORGET ✳

In 1947 national teams were still used in the Tour de France but Germany, with the events of the Second World War still fresh in the mind of a ravaged France, was not invited to enter a team and wouldn't be for another decade. The Italian team was made up of Franco-Italians living in France and as with the French nation's attitude towards Germany, it was deemed too sensitive an issue to permit an Italian national team to ride in the Tour.

✳ THE FLEA ✳

Vicente Trueba, nicknamed "The Flea of Torrelavega", took part in the Tour de France during the 1930s. He weighed just over 45kg (about seven stones), which meant he could fly up the mountains but sadly lacked the body weight to come down at high speed. Despite reaching the top of the mountain climbs before many of the racing greats at the time, he never won a Tour de France stage.

✳ BIKES NUMBERED ✳

For the 1914 Tour de France, in addition to the numbers on the riders' jerseys, race numbers were also fixed to the riders' bikes.

❋ TOUR LEGENDS (8) – MIGUEL INDURAIN ❋

Miguel Indurain was born on 16 July 1964 in Villava, Navarre, Spain. He began his professional racing career in 1985, making his Tour de France debut that year, but abandoned after four stages. A year later, Miguel abandoned after Stage 8 of the Tour, but did win his first professional race, the 1986 Tour de l'Avenir. However, his Tour de France performances improved year to year, going from 97th in 1987 to 10th in 1990. And he might have won the 1990 Tour but he was under orders to assist his Banesto team-leader, Pedro Delgado, the 1988 winner.

Miguel enjoyed success in other events, winning the 1988 Tour of Catalonia, the 1989 Critérium International – the first-ever Spaniard to do so – and the prestigious Paris–Nice in 1989. In 1990 he retained his Paris–Nice title and also won the Clasica San Sebastian–San Sebastian, a race traditionally dominated by climbers. Throughout his career, "Big Mig" utterly dominated Tour opponents in individual time trials (ITT). In fact, only two of Indurain's 12 Tour stage wins were not *contre-la-montre* – and, surprisingly, they were both in the mountains. His first stage win had come in 1989, from Pau to Cauterets in the Pyrenees, after which he wore the polka dot jersey (King of the Mountains), but it was for the only day of his Tour career, and he eventually finished 17th in the general classification. The second mountain stage victory came climbing up to Luz Ardiden in 1990.

Indurain entered the 1991 Tour in magnificent form and won his first Tour, thanks largely to two dominant performances in ITT. In the 1992 Tour, Indurain took the 65km ITT in Luxembourg by an incredible three minutes. In addition to winning the Tour in both 1992 and 1993 he also claimed the Giro d'Italia. With his fourth consecutive Tour victory in 1994, Indurain moved into select company and added to his legacy by setting a World Hour Record (53.040km) that year. Miguel claimed the Critérium du Dauphiné Libéré in 1995 (he would repeat the feat in 1996), and reached the summit of cycling, joining Jacques Anquetil, Eddy Merckx and Bernard Hinault as five-time Tour de France winners.

In 1996, Indurain attempted to create Tour history by becoming the first man to win six times. However, he contracted bronchitis, which in effect ended his dreams of Tour immortality and he finished 11th overall behind Denmark's first-ever winner, Bjarne Riis. In September 1996, Indurain surprisingly abandoned the Vuelta a España, just 19km from the finish of a stage.

Did You Know That?
During the Atlanta 1996 Olympic Games, Indurain won gold medal in the Individual Time Trial.

✳ TOUR SPOKESMEN (35) ✳

"I'm not going for stage wins, just the 'most elegant rider' and 'most unfortunate rider's' prizes."
Tom Simpson, former pro cyclist on the Tour de France in 1967

✳ OLD LEGS ✳

The following riders all won the Tour de France after their 32nd birthday.
1903: Maurice Garin, 32
1919: Firmin Lambot, 33
1921: Léon Scieur, 33
1922: Firmin Lambot, 36
1923: Henri Pélissier, 34
1926: Lucien Buysse, 34
1929: Maurice Dewaele, 33
1948: Gino Bartali, 34
1952: Fausto Coppi, 33
1980: Joop Zoetemelk, 33
1996: Bjarne Riis, 32
2004: Lance Armstrong, 32*
2005: Lance Armstrong, 33*
2011: Cadel Evans, 34
2012: Bradley Wiggins, 32
* *Subsequently stripped of the title.*

✳ THE THREE PELISSIER BROTHERS ✳

There were three outstanding cycling Pélissier brothers: Charles, Francis and Henri. Charles, the youngest, won stages in four different Tours (16 in total, in 1929, 1930, 1931 and 1932). Francis won Paris–Tours, the French Championship, Bordeaux–Paris and stages in two different Tours de France, but only managed to finish the 1923 race. However, the best of the three brothers was the oldest, Henri, who claimed 10 stage victories in the two Tours de France in which he competed and won the 1923 Tour. Henri also won Milan–Turin, Milan–San Remo, Tour of Lombardy, Paris–Roubaix, Paris–Brussels, Paris–Tours and the Tour of the Basque Country.

❋ A GERMAN JUDAS ❋

Stage 16 of the 2004 Tour de France was an exciting individual time trial up l'Alpe d'Huez. Lance Armstrong's (US Postal) ride was as superb as it was devastating, winning the stage and gaining time in the yellow jersey which he retained all the way to Paris to win his sixth consecutive Tour (although, in 2012, he was stripped of all his Tour wins). He beat Jan Ullrich (T-Mobile) by 61 seconds and caught Ivan Basso (CSC), who had started the stage two minutes in front of him, with four kilometres to go. Somewhere in the region of 750,000 people lined the stage route, and many of the German fans booed their countryman Jens Voigt (CSC), who had been instrumental in chasing down Jan Ullrich the day before. Placards were waved castigating Voigt, including several which called him "Judas". After the stage was over, Ullrich found himself defending Voigt during a press conference, saying that the CSC rider was only doing his job for his team.

❋ CHAMP CALLS IT A DAY ❋

Bernard Hinault decided not to ride in the 1987 Tour de France, feeling he could no longer ride at cycling's top levels, and subsequently retired. He rode his last professional race in November 1986.

❋ 12-STAGE WINNER WHO NEVER SAW PARIS ❋

Italian sprint ace Mario Cipollini (GB-MG) won Stage 1 of the 1993 Tour de France, the first of 12 career stage victories in the race. Amazingly, despite riding in eight Tours, the mountains always proved too much for him and he failed to complete any of them.

❋ A MAJOR PILE-UP ❋

On Stage 2 of the 1999 Tour de France there was a 25-rider pile-up at Passage du Gois. Passage du Gois is actually a 3.5km causeway which, depending on the tide, can at certain times be under water.

❋ UNLUCKY THIRTEENTH ❋

On Stage 15 of the 1975 Tour de France, on 13 July, the Bianchi team car trying to keep up with Felice Gimondi flew off the side of the road coming down the Allos. The team mechanic was thrown from the car and landed in a tree, and the driver, Giancarlo Ferretti, was lucky to survive the 45-metre drop.

✳ GUIMARD IN YELLOW ✳

Stage 1 of the 1972 Tour de France was won by Cyrille Guimard, a member of Raymond Poulidor's Gan-Mercier team. With the stage victory and time bonus the young Guimard took the yellow jersey, ahead of Eddy Merckx by a narrow 7 seconds. Merckx won his fourth consecutive Tour de France that year, while Guimard went on to be a very successful team manager after he quit racing professionally.

✳ THE RUSSIANS ARE COMING ✳

In 1990, a Russian team entered the Tour de France for the first time in the race's 87-year history. The riders were sponsored by Alfa-Lum and performed well, Dmitri Konyshev winning Stage 17. Two other riders on the Alfa-Lum team would go on to do well on the European professional circuit over the next few years: Piotr Ugramov and Djamolidine Abdujaparov.

✳ TRIPLE EXIT ✳

Stephen Roche was unable to defend the *maillot jaune* he had won the previous year when the 1988 Tour de France came around. The Irishman had undergone two knee operations between his World Championship win and the start of the new season. Greg LeMond, the 1986 Tour winner, was still recovering from his hunting accident and although the double champion from the 1983 and 1984 Tours, Laurent Fignon, started the 1988 Tour, he was forced to abandon it after Stage 11. The triple exit paved the way for Pedro Delgado, who had been runner-up to Roche in 1987 by 40 seconds, to win the 1988 Tour de France.

✳ ANQUETIL THE MOUNTAIN GOAT ✳

Jacques Anquetil was never considered a great climber and often rode conservatively during the mountain stages of the Tour de France before blowing the field away in the individual time trial stages. However, in Stage 10 of the 1963 Tour, a 148.5-kilometre trek that took the riders over the Aubisque and the Tourmalet, Anquetil claimed his first-ever mountain stage victory. The win surprised the media, who now found themselves writing about an Anquetil who could trade pedal-strokes with specialist climbers on their own turf, and then fly past them in the sprint to the finish. Not surprisingly, Anquetil won the 1963 Tour de France.

❋ GREAT CLIMBS (8) – COL DU TOURMALET ❋

The most-climbed mountain in Tour de France history, the Col du Tourmalet appeared in every one from 1910 to 1955, except for 1922. To reach the summit, riders must climb the highest road in the central Pyrenees. *L'Auto* journalist Adolphe Steines visited the Pyrenees in 1910 and reported back to Paris that climbs in the mountains were viable. The legend of the Tourmalet goes back more than 100 years, including Octave Lapize's rant at organisers in 1910 and, three years later, Eugène Christophe's adventures in the Sainte-Marie de Campan forge repairing the forks he broke on the mountain.

Location: The département of Haute-Pyrenées in SE France, close to the Andorra and Spain borders.

Nearest town: La Mongie.

Height: 2,115m.

Gradient: From Luz-Saint-Sauveur in the west, the climb is 1,404m over 19km, an average gradient of 7.4 percent, but 10.2 percent at the summit; from Sainte-Marie de Campan, the climb is 17.2km, rising 1,268m, also an average gradient of 7.4 percent, with a maximum of 10 percent.

Characteristics: Two memorials can be found on the summit. One is to Jacques Goddet, director of the Tour from 1936 to 1987, the other to the first man to cross the summit, Octave Lapize, who is depicted gasping for air as he struggles near the peak.

Tour visits: 79 in total. In 1970 and 1974, the Tourmalet was climbed twice, though in the former's case the first stage finish was at 1,770m-high La Mongie. In both 1974 and 2010, the stage finished at the summit.

Multiple winners: 4: Federico Bahamontes (1954, 1962, 1963*, 1964*); 3: Lucien Van Impe (1971, 1975, 1977), Julio Jiminez (1964*, 1965, 1967); 2: Firmin Lambot (1914, 1920), Benoit Fauré (1930, 1932), Sylvère Maes (1935, 1936), Jean Robic (1947, 1948), Fausto Coppi (1949, 1952), Richard Virenque (1994 1995), Alberto Elli (1998, 1999).

* = *Two riders were ruled to have crossed the summit together.*

Conquerors of the peak: Bernard Thévenet (1970), Jean-Pierre Danguillaume (1974) and Andy Schleck (2010) won stages finishing on the Col du Tourmalet.

Did You Know That?
The first time the Tour visited the high mountains it was the Pyrenees in 1910 and not the Alps. When Octave Lapize reached the summit of Le Tourmalet in 1910, he screamed at the Tour organisers, "You are murderers, yes murderers!"

❋ DOUBLE CENTURY WINNER ❋

In 1914, Philippe Thys (Belgium) became the first rider to win the Tour de France in a time exceeding 200 hours. He completed the anticlockwise Pyrenees-first Tour, comprising 15 stages covering 5,405 kilometres, in 200 hours 28 minutes 49 seconds.

❋ THREE NEW CLIMBS ❋

In 1952 a new climb was introduced to the Tour de France: Puy de Dôme. Two new summits were also added: l'Alpe d'Huez and Sestriere. All three climbs were to be hilltop finishes, with Puy de Dôme being a steep climb up an extinct volcano in France's Massif Central. Today a stage finish at the top of a mountain is a standard part of every Tour de France but they were only introduced to the race in 1951.

❋ TOUR SPOKESMEN (36) ❋

"I climb cols [mountains] by feel and I don't look at my heart meter. That said, I do have a look at my rivals' heart meters sometimes, to see what state they're in."
Richard Virenque, seven-time Tour de France King of the Mountains

❋ SEVEN TOUR WINNERS ❋

In 1925, Automoto brought a truly formidable team to the Tour de France. Between them the six riders on the team had won five Tours: Ottavio Bottecchia (1924), Lucien and Jules Buysse, Francis and Henri Pélissier (1923) plus Philippe Thys (1913, 1914, 1920). Bottecchia won his second overall jersey in 1925, while Lucien Buysse won the Tour in 1926.

✳ REVOLUTIONARY BARS ✳

Stage 5 of the 1989 Tour de France witnessed a new revolution in individual time trial racing. Greg LeMond (ADR) won the stage using his new triathlon bars, which helped narrow his frontal profile. LeMond finished the 73-kilometre course in a time of 1 hour 38 minutes 12 seconds, with Pedro Delgado (Reynolds-Banesto) in second place at 24 seconds and Laurent Fignon (Super U) third at 56 seconds.

✳ TOUR SPOKESMEN (37) ✳

"It was so hot that the tar was melting under our tyres. I was completely drained and dehydrated. I ended up stopping beside a farm and I lapped up the dirty water from the cattle trough. And that's how I got foot-and-mouth disease. It's usually only cows that get that!"
Raphaël Géminiani, former pro cyclist and 1951 Tour de France King of the Mountains

✳ RIDER BREAKS HIS BACK IN FALL ✳

On Stage 14 of the 1960 Tour de France Roger Rivière (France) crashed into a ravine on the descent of the Col du Perjuret. Rivière broke his back in the fall and was unable to ride a bike ever again. It was suggested that he crashed because he could not feel his brake levers as a result of the cocktail of amphetamines, painkillers and sleeping pills in his body. Rivière was a three-times World Pursuit Champion; he had set the World Hour Record in 1957 and then bettered it in 1958. Indeed, his 1958 World Hour Record was so good that it stood for a decade. Gastone Nencini (Italy) won the Tour in 1960 and gave the winners' bouquet of flowers to Marcel Bidot, the French team manager, to give to Rivière.

✳ TOUR VISITS HELL OF THE NORTH ✳

Stage 9 of the 1979 Tour de France was a ride over the "Hell of the North", the tough cobblestone streets and roads of northern France with a finish in the famous Roubaix Velodrome. Bernard Hinault, the 1978 Tour winner, rode into the velodrome in a group that included Hennie Kuiper, Lucien Van Impe and Giovanni Battaglin 3 minutes and 45 seconds after Joop Zoetemelk. Zoetemelk took the leader's yellow jersey from a tearful Hinault.

❋ CARRY ON RIDING ❋

During Stage 13 of the 2004 Tour de France Iban Mayo (Euskaltel-Euskadi) attempted to quit the race as he was finding the mountains difficult. He got off his bike, but was persuaded by his team manager to get back in the saddle. Still suffering, he took his feet off the pedals while his teammates encouraged him not to give up. At one point even Fabian Cancellara of the Fassa Bortolo team rode alongside him, urging the Spaniard along. Mayo eventually finished the stage, 38 minutes behind the winner, but he quit the Tour after Stage 14. Almost 50 years earlier (1956) a fellow Spaniard, Federico Bahamontes, dramatically quit the Tour when he threw his bike down a ravine.

❋ SUBS INTRODUCED ❋

For the 1928 Tour de France the Tour boss Henri Desgrange retained his time-trial format and permitted teams to replace a rider if necessary. Indeed, five replacement riders entered the lists and rode in the Tour when their teammates were unable to continue.

❋ FIRST STOP GERMANY ❋

In 1965 the Tour de France started in Germany for the first time in the Tour's 62-year history. Rik Van Looy won the Cologne–Liège stage and the 1965 Tour de France's first *maillot jaune*.

❋ A MOUNTAINOUS TOUR ❋

The 1976 Tour was mountainous in more ways than one. The Tour started on France's west coast and then circled north up to Belgium before heading south to the Alps. In previous Tours, after the riders climbed either the Alps or the Pyrenees several transition stages came into play before the next set of climbs. However in 1976, stages 7–11 were all Alp climbs followed by a rest-day before stages 12–14 took the riders straight into the Pyrenees. Eight consecutive mountain stages was unheard of and to cap this, Stage 20 finished at the top of Puy de Dôme. No fewer than five of the mountain stages ended with hilltop finishes. Not surprisingly Lucien Van Impe, King of the Mountains in 1971, 1972 and 1975, announced his intention to claim the overall yellow jersey in 1976 and the Belgian did not disappoint his Gitane-Campagnolo team or his fans.

❊ GREAT TOURS DE FRANCE (8): 1978 ❊

It was the start of a new era in 1978, following the retirement of Eddy Merckx, Felice Gimondi, Raymond Poulidor and Luis Ocaña. Lucien Van Impe, the 1976 winner, competed, but he was still recovering from a broken collarbone he suffered a few weeks earlier. The two favourites were Bernard Hinault of France and Joop Zoetemelk of the Netherlands. When race leader Michel Pollentier was disqualified for giving a fake doping sample (he had hidden a bottle with a clean sample attached to his leg), Zoetemelk took over in yellow, but he lost out to better time triallist Hinault on Stage 20, a 72km (45-mile) battle *contre-la-montre*. Hinault took more than four minutes out of Zoetemelk, enough to ensure he won the Tour – his first – by 3' 56".

Rank	Name	Country	Time
1.	Bernard Hinault	France	107h 18' 00"
2.	Joop Zoetemelk	Netherlands	+3' 56"
3.	Joaquim Agostinho	Portugal	+6' 54"
4.	Joseph Bruyère	Belgium	+9' 04"
5.	Christian Seznec	France	+12' 50"
6.	Paul Wellens	Belgium	+14' 38"
7.	Francisco Galdos	Spain	+17' 08"
8.	Henk Lubberding	Netherlands	+17' 26"
9.	Lucien Van Impe	Belgium	+21' 01"
10.	Mariano Martinez	France	+22' 58"

Did You Know That?
The first part of Stage 1 finished in Sint Willebrord, the home town of the first Dutchman to wear the yellow jersey, Wim Van Est. Jan Raas, also of the Netherlands – who had won the Prologue on Leiden a day before – claimed the stage.

❊ A CORPSE WINS THE TOUR ❊

Prior to Stage 15 of the 1929 Tour de France, the Alcyon team requested and was granted a one-hour delay before starting the stage because their rider Maurice De Waele (Belgium), who was also overall leader in the GC, was still asleep in bed. De Waele had been unwell before Stage 14 and was unable to eat solids. However, his teammates helped him to the end of Stage 15 and nursed him all the way to Paris where he claimed the overall yellow jersey, much to the annoyance of Henri Desgrange, who announced "a corpse has won my race".

✻ BIKE MANUFACTURERS TEAM UP ✻

As a result of the terrible conditions and mass shortages in post-First World War France, bike manufacturers were unable to individually sponsor teams in the 1919 Tour de France as they had done before the war. Consequently they joined forces to equip about half of the peloton under the name "La Sportive".

✻ THIRD ACROSS THE LINE WINS STAGE ✻

Stage 18 of the 1977 Tour de France was overshadowed by serious doping problems. The first riders to cross the line, Joaquim Agostinho and Antonio Menendez, were relegated after testing positive while Eddy Merckx, who had crossed the finishing line in third place, was awarded the stage victory.

✻ WATER BOTTLE PUTS ROBIC IN YELLOW ✻

In the 1953 Tour de France Jean Robic, winner of the first post-war Tour in 1947, wasn't riding for the French national team – he was a member of the regional team France-Ouest, managed by Léon Le Calvez (a former rider with the French national team during the 1930s). Although Robic was an outstanding rider, he was simply unable to descend at speed given his small size – 1.52m (5 feet) – and lack of weight. The evening before Stage 9, which took the riders into the Pyrenees, Le Calvez poured molten lead into a water bottle, which in those days were made from aluminium. At the top of the climb the bottle was secretly passed to Robic who then had an extra 9kg of weight to aid his descent. The handover had to be carried out in secret because handing a rider food or water could be done only at a designated feed zone. With his new water bottle on board Robic had effectively doubled the weight of his bike as he quickly made his descent. By the time Robic descended the Tourmalet in Stage 11 he was able to get down the mountain quickly enough to stay away from the peloton and claim the yellow jersey despite the fact that he hadn't even been in the top five placings of the general classification after Stage 9. It would be the last of his six career Tour de France stage wins.

✻ PASSPORTS AT THE READY ✻

The 1974 Tour de France took the riders from France to England to Belgium, back into France, and then on to Spain before re-entering France.

✷ THE COMPLETE RIDER ✷

Fausto Coppi won all there was to win in professional cycling: the World Hour Record, the World Championships, Grand Tours, Classics and Time Trials. Such was Coppi's dominance of the sport that the great French cycling journalist Pierre Chany once wrote that between 1946 and 1954, as soon as Coppi broke away from a peloton, the peloton was incapable of catching him.

✷ TOUR SPOKESMEN (38) ✷

"The Tour de France is finished and the second edition will, I fear, also be the last. It has died of its success, of the blind passions that it unleashed, the abuse and the dirty suspicions ... We will therefore leave it to others to take the chance of taking on an adventure in the Tour de France."
Henri Desgrange, founder of the Tour de France

✷ THE WIEL'S AFFAIR ✷

Stage 14 of the 1962 Tour de France was to take the riders from Superbagnères over the Ares and the Portet d'Aspet mountains, finishing with a climb up to the fortified city of Carcassonne. Hans Junkermann, riding for the Wiel's team, had been very ill the night before the stage started. Team Wiel's requested and was granted a delay to the start of the stage for their team captain, who lay in seventh place overall in the general classification. When the peloton finally set off it was clear that Junkermann was incapable of continuing and he was forced to abandon the race. He claimed that fish he ate in his hotel the night before had caused his illness. By the end of the stage 14 riders, including three of Junkermann's teammates, were also forced to abandon the Tour through illness. A total of eight teams had been affected by the withdrawals, but when questioned about the riders' illness the hotel claimed that they had not served anyone fish the night before the stage. The day had been very hot and many journalists at the time believed that a doping exercise had simply gone wrong; indeed one cartoonist drew a picture of the riders at their dinner table with syringes replacing the fish bones. When the riders saw the newspapers and what was being implied, they threatened to go on strike but Louison Bobet's brother Jean managed to convince them that a strike would only make the situation worse. The incident is known today as the "Wiel's Affair".

❋ FIRST WINNERS BY COUNTRY ❋

Year	Country	Cyclist
1903	France	Maurice Garin
1909	Luxembourg	François Faber
1913	Belgium	Odile Defraye
1924	Italy	Ottavio Bottechia
1950	Switzerland	Ferdinand Kübler
1959	Spain	Federico Bahamontes
1968	Netherlands	Jan Janssen
1986	USA	Greg LeMond
1987	Ireland	Stephen Roche
1996	Denmark	Bjarne Riis
1997	Germany	Jan Ullrich
2011	Australia	Cadel Evans
2012	Great Britain	Bradley Wiggins

❋ TOUR DEATHS (3) ❋

Italy's Fabio Casartelli crashed in the rain descending the Col de Portet d'Aspet, Stage 15 of the 1995 Tour de France. An Olympic Games gold medallist at Barcelona 1992, he wasn't wearing a helmet when he struck his head on concrete blocks and died of his injuries.

❋ STAGE ANNULLED ❋

Stage 12 of the 1978 Tour de France was scheduled to have two sections. The riders were required to get up at 5am after an exhausting, monumental stage the previous day and after riding slowly in protest at the early start they were one and a half hours behind the Tour's planned schedule. When the peloton reached the finish line in the little French town of Valence d'Agen, the riders stopped, dismounted and, led by Bernard Hinault, simply walked across the line in protest. The town's residents were furious that their six months of preparation for the stage finish, in addition to the fees they paid the Tour's organisers, were wasted. The stage was annulled.

❋ *MAILLOT JAUNE* ABSENT ❋

Fausto Coppi was not able to ride in the 1950 Tour de France to defend the yellow jersey he had won the previous year, as he was still recovering from a bad Giro d'Italia crash that resulted in a broken pelvis.

❋ TOUR SPOKESMEN (39) ❋

"I was a hero, and a second afterwards it was all over. Casartelli was dead so what I had achieved was nothing."
Richard Virenque, on winning a Tour de France stage in which Fabio Casartelli died in a crash

❋ HELICOPTER FOR POULIDOR ❋

Stage 13 of the 1973 Tour de France involved four huge Pyrenean climbs en route to the finish line: the Puymorens, the Portet d'Aspet, the Col de Mente and the Portillon. On his way down the Portet d'Aspet Raymond Poulidor crashed and had to be taken off the mountain to hospital by helicopter. His Tour was over. Luis Ocaña claimed a clear solo victory.

❋ 50TH ANNIVERSARY TOUR ❋

In 1953 the Tour de France celebrated its 50th anniversary, and to mark the occasion a new competition was introduced, the Green Jersey for the best sprinter. Originally called the Grand Prix Cinquentenaire, points were awarded to the best-placed finishers after each day's stage. The competition has been refined over the last half-century as the modern-day Tour awards more points to the flat than to the mountain stages, to emphasise that it is an award designed for the speed merchants in the pack.

❋ UNRELATED BACK-TO-BACK WINS ❋

In the 1936 Tour de France, Belgium fielded a superb team starting with the previous year's winner, Romain Maes, plus Sylvère Maes (no relation to Romain), who had ridden in the 1935 Tour as a Belgian *individuel* and finished fourth, Félicien Vervaecke and Marcel Kint (The Black Eagle). Sylvère Maes won the 1936 Tour de France.

❋ THE GERMAN MASTER ❋

Jan Ullrich's victory in the 1997 Tour de France, the 84th to be held, made him the first German rider to win cycling's greatest prize. Ullrich, participating in only his second Tour de France after finishing runner-up in the 1996 Tour, also became the first rider since Laurent Fignon in 1983 to claim a simultaneous victory in both the General Classification and the *maillot blanc* young riders category.

✻ TIME BONUSES INTRODUCED ✻

In the 1923 Tour de France, Henri Desgrange introduced time bonuses for stage wins. To encourage the riders to improve their efforts to claim a stage victory, 2 minutes were removed from the elapsed time of the winner of each stage. In the 2006, a time bonus of 20 seconds was awarded to each stage winner, 12 seconds for second and 8 seconds for third.

✻ COPPI SAYS "NO" ✻

Fausto Coppi refused to ride for the Italian team in the 1948 Tour de France. Many writers put it down to the fact that Coppi and Gino Bartali, for whom Coppi had once been a *domestique*, did not get along, but others cited what happened to Coppi in the 1948 Giro d'Italia as the underpinning reason for his absence from the Tour. Coppi abandoned the Giro before Stage 18 after winning the 16th and 17th stages, both mountain stages. A man of high principles and integrity, Coppi was most sensitive to any sort of preference or favouritism offered to his competitors at his expense. In the 1948 Giro Coppi was of the opinion that the judges assisted Fiorenzo Magni's cheating; the judges had given Magni nominal penalties which did nothing to negate the advantage he gained breaking the race rules. And so, just as the Belgian team abandoned the 1937 Tour de France after Roger Lapébie's obvious cheating, Coppi quit rather than be defrauded.

✻ A SPANIARD IN PARIS ✻

Luis Ocaña had an excellent 1973, winning the Tour of the Basque Country, the Catalonian Week, the Dauphiné Libéré and a runner-up spot to Eddy Merckx in the Vuelta a España, but his greatest prize of all that year was the overall *maillot jaune* in the 1973 Tour de France. He became Spain's first Tour de France winner since Federico Bahamontes took top spot on the podium in Paris in 1959.

✻ A COSTLY HELPING HAND ✻

During Stage 4 of the 1993 Tour de France, an 81-kilometre team time trial won by the GB-MG team which included Mario Cipolini, the riders on the Clas Team had given each other pushes along the way and were handed a one-minute penalty. It meant that Toni Rominger and his teammates lost a total of 3 minutes 6 seconds overall.

❋ TOUR LEGENDS (9) – LANCE ARMSTRONG ❋

Lance Armstrong was born Lance Edward Gunderson in Plano, Texas, USA, on 18 September 1971. He started his sporting career as a triathlete and competed in adult competitions aged just 14. At 17 he received an invitation to train with the USA Junior National Cycling Team but his school objected. With his mother's approval Lance withdrew from school and joined the National Cycling Team.

An outstanding amateur cyclist, he won the US amateur championship in 1991 and finished 14th in the 1992 Olympic Games Cycling Road Race after which he turned professional. In 1993 Lance secured his first major victory, winning the World Cycling Championships in Oslo. In 1993 Lance competed in his maiden Tour de France, riding for the Motorola team, and won Stage 8, before abandoning after 12 stages. Armstrong had a good 1995, winning several classic one-day events including the Tour DuPont and the Clásica de San Sebastián. He also won a second Tour stage in the Tour de France, Stage 18, on his way to 36th overall. In 1996 he abandoned the Tour for the third time in four attempts, but did win La Flèche Wallonne.

On 2 October 1996 Armstrong's world was thrown into turmoil when he was diagnosed with stage-three testicular cancer that had also spread to his brain and lungs. The doctors gave him less than a 40 percent chance of survival and at one stage this success rate was as low as 3 percent. Armstrong never gave up hope of a full recovery and despite having his right testicle and two brain lesions removed he made a remarkable recovery. Cofidis coldly terminated Armstrong's contract with the team, but in 1998 he joined the newly formed US Postal team. His first Grand Tour event for US Postal was the 1998 Vuelta a España and he finished fourth in the general classification.

In 1999 Lance won four stages in the Tour and claimed his first winners' *maillot jaune* in Paris. Armstrong won the next Tours and retired from professional cycling after his seventh Tour de France success. Outside racing he worked alongside his sponsor, Nike, and in 1997 founded "The Lance Armstrong Foundation" to raise money across the globe to help fight cancer, most visibly via the famous yellow "Livestrong" wrist band.

In 2008, Lance returned to competitive cycling, finishing third in the 2009 Tour de France and 23rd the following year. In February 2011, he again announced his retirement from cycling.

Did You Know That?
All of Lance Armstrong's Tour de France achievements were nullified after a long investigation into doping. Tour organisers have decided not to reassign any of his 22 Tour de France stage wins or seven general classification victories to other riders.

✻ BARTALI AND COPPI SUSPENDED ✻

Prior to the 1949 Tour de France, in which Gino Bartali and Fausto Coppi both rode for the Italian national team, the pair let their intense rivalry get the better of them at the 1948 World Championships at Valkenburg, Holland. During the race Bartali and Coppi merely shadowed one another, a move which then permitted lesser riders to speed ahead of them. When they realised that they were too far behind the leader and eventual winner, Rik Van Steenbergen of Belgium, to be in contention, they both quit. After the race a furious Italian Cycling Federation, angry that the pair had allowed their rivalry to override their responsibilities as members of the Italian team, gave Bartali and Coppi a symbolic (it was the end of the season) three-month suspension.

✻ TOUR BOMBED ✻

Stages 15 and 16 of the 1974 Tour de France took the riders into Spain where Basque separatists bombed some of the team and press cars. Vicente López Carril, the reigning Spanish Champion, wore his Kas team colours (blue and green) over the two days rather than wear Spanish colours and run the risk of being targeted by the terrorists.

✻ PEUGEOT DOMINANT ✻

The Peugeot team that entered the 1908 Tour de France included some of the greatest riders of the time: Hippolyte Aucouturier, Lucien Petit-Breton (1907 winner), Henri Cornet (1904 winner), François Faber, Gustave Garrigou and Emile Georget. Between them the Peugeot team members had already won over 20 stage wins during the previous five Tours. So dominant were the Peugeot riders that no other team managed to win any of the 14 stages. Lucien Petit-Breton rode to victory with 36 points with his teammate François Faber in second place on 68 points, while two other Peugeot riders (Georges Passerieu and Gustave Garrigou) occupied the remaining two places in the top four.

❊ EIGHT MEN IN YELLOW ❊

The 1987 Tour de France, won by Ireland's Stephen Roche, was a superb spectacle of racing with eight different men wearing the yellow jersey, a Tour de France record.

❊ THE OLD GAUL ❊

Stage 6 of the 1913 Tour de France is one of the greatest ever in the history of the race and enjoys iconic status. The stage, which included crossings of the Aubisque, Tourmalet, Aspin and Peyresourde, covered 326 kilometres from Bayonne to Luchon and took the winner 14 hours to complete. Following an early crash the defending Tour champion Odile Defraye (Belgium) found himself over two hours behind the leading riders and abandoned the race when he got to Barèges at the foot of the Tourmalet. Eugène Christophe, nicknamed "Le Vieux Gaulois" (the Old Gaul), and Philippe Thys were leading the stage but when they climbed the Tourmalet Thys pulled away and managed a five-minute lead over his rival at the top of the climb. A little way down the descent of the Tourmalet, Christophe broke the fork on his bike. In the early Tours riders had to fix their own bikes, cars following with a replacement bike being some years away yet. Christophe placed his bike over his shoulder and carried the broken fork and front wheel in his other hand as he ran down the remaining 10 kilometres of the valley to St-Marie-de-Campan. When he reached the small town Christophe approached a little girl who guided him to Monsieur Lecomte's blacksmith's shop, where Christophe, a skilled mechanic, repaired his fork under the supervision of one of Desgrange's race commissars. It took Christophe over three hours to fix his broken fork and despite being exhausted after his long ordeal he got back on his bike and set off for Luchon with the Aspin and the Peyresourde climbs still ahead of him. However, just as he left the blacksmith's shop he was informed by the commissar that he had incurred a 10-minute penalty because a little seven-year-old boy named Corni had helped him with his repair by working the bellows (the penalty was subsequently reduced to 3 minutes). Thys won the stage, while Christophe came in 3 hours 50 minutes 14 seconds behind him in 29th place. Amazingly, despite having to run for 10 kilometres and spending three hours fixing his broken fork, Christophe still managed to cross the finish line ahead of 15 other riders. Today a plaque can be found on the building where the blacksmith's shop used to be.

❋ TOUR SPOKESMEN (40) ❋

"I'm fascinated by sprinters, they suffer so much during the race just to get to the finish, they hang on for dear life on the climbs, but then in the final kilometres they are transformed and do amazing things. It's not their force per se that impresses me, but rather the renaissance they experience. Seeing them suffer throughout the race only to be reborn in the final is something for fascination."
Tom Simpson, former pro cyclist on the Tour de France in 1967

❋ THE PRODIGY ❋

Léon Scieur, winner of the 1921 Tour de France, was a discovery of the 1919 and 1922 Tour winner Firmin Lambot. Lambot persuaded Scieur to become a professional cyclist with both men coming from Florennes, a small French-speaking village in Wallonia, Belgium.

❋ DESGRANGE MELLOWS ❋

In 1909 Henri Desgrange abandoned his 1908 requirement that all riders should compete on Tour-supplied frames; the teams were henceforth allowed to ride their own bikes. However, Tour officials stamped all bikes entered in the 1909 Tour to ensure that the riders started and finished with the same machine.

❋ PAST MASTER CRASHES OUT ❋

Jean Robic, winner of the Tour de France in 1947, was forced to abandon the 1954 Tour after a bad crash on Stage 4b.

❋ VUELTA A ESPANA CHAMP TAKES YELLOW ❋

Rudi Altig from Germany, winner of the Vuelta a España in the spring of 1962, won the opening stage of the 1962 Tour de France. Altig was a member of Jacques Anquetil's very strong St Raphaël-Halyett team.

❋ AFTER YOU BROTHER ❋

Henri Pélissier (Automoto) won Stage 3 of the 1923 Tour de France, a 405-kilometre journey that took the riders from Cherbourg to Brest, while his brother Francis, also an Automoto rider, finished second with the same time.

❋ GREAT CLIMBS (9) – LUZ ARDIDEN ❋

The Luz Ardiden is a recent addition to the Tour de France, having made its debut in 1985, since when it has appeared seven further times. The construction of a ski station in the late 1970s and the construction of a road up the mountain made it a viable ascent for Tour riders. The road out of Luz-Saint-Sauveur offers two iconic climbs because a left turn will take the riders up the Col de Tourmalet; to the right Luz Ardiden is less than 15km away. Unusually, and maybe because of the ski resort there, Luz Ardiden has always been a stage finish.

Location: The département of Haute-Pyrénées, and region of Midi-Pyrénées in southern France.

Nearest town: Luz-Saint-Sauveur.

Height: The peak is 2,500m, but the stage summit is at the ski resort, 1,720m.

Gradient: The average gradient of the ascent is 6.9 percent, being 1,010m over 14.7km, but the maximum gradient is 10 percent.

Characteristics: The climb from Luz-Saint-Sauveur is relatively short, but it is very tough, with numerous twists and turns in the road. Unusually, the steepest part of the ascent comes around halfway up the road, rather than up to the summit itself.

Tour visits: 8.

Multiple winners: None.

Conquerors of the peak: Pedro Delgado (1985), Dag Otto Lauritzen (1987), Laudelino Cubino Gonzalez (1988), Miguel Indurain (1990*), Richard Virenque (1994), Roberto Laiseka (2001), None** (2003), Samuel Sanchez (2011).

* = Claudio Chiappucci won the stage. ** = Lance Armstrong was stripped of his stage win.

Did You Know That?
Lance Armstrong and Iban Mayo, riding together, crashed at the start of the climb up Luz Ardiden in 2003 after Armstrong's handlebars tangled with the handbag of a spectator standing at the side of the road.

✿ TOUR SPOKESMEN (41) ✿

"Yorkshire is a region of outstanding beauty, with breathtaking landscapes whose terrains offer both sprinters and attackers the opportunity to express themselves."
Christian Prudhomme, Tour Director, on Yorkshire hosting the 2014 Grand Départ

✿ THE BERNINA STRIKE ✿

The Italian Cycling Federation did not enter a team in the 1954 Tour de France as a direct result of the "Bernina Strike" in that year's Giro d'Italia. The Giro organisers paid Fausto Coppi a huge sum as his presence was important to the event's success. However, other riders were resentful that *Il Campionissimo* was given such preferential treatment. It went wrong quickly when Coppi became very ill after eating a plate of oysters following the opening stage. He lost 11½ minutes in Stage 2 and was clearly unable to ride his normal race. Giuseppe Ambrosini, the Giro director, asked the riders to save the race by riding aggressively. Fiorenzo Magni along with a few others took up the baton and raced hard throughout Stage 3, believing their efforts would earn them a generous financial reward from Ambrosini. But they were disappointed with their meagre payment so, in Stage 4, they took things more easily and refusing to race hard. Their refusal to compete against each other resulted in a Swiss team *domestique*, Carlo Clerici, getting himself into a breakaway group in Stage 6 which led the field, including Coppi, by more than 30 minutes and placed him in the leader's pink jersey. Three stages from the end, Coppi clawed a lot of time back on Clerici and, now fit again, race organisers believed they would now get the race they desired. However it didn't turn out that way, as Coppi and the peloton, still in dispute, rode easily over the Bernina pass which allowed Clerici to claim overall victory. When the race entered the Vigorelli Velodrome in Milan, the derisive whistles from the crowd were so loud that the riders couldn't hear the bell signalling the final lap. The Italian Cycling Federation was furious, and handed Coppi a two-month suspension as well as boycotting the Tour de France.

✿ A COSTLY DRINK OF WATER ✿

Jean Roussius, winner of Stage 1 in the 1919 Tour de France, was given a 30-minute penalty for giving Philippe Thys a drink of water.

✳ WHITE JERSEY WINNERS ✳

Year	Winner	Country
1975	Francesco Moser	Italy
1976	Enrique Martinez-Heredia	Spain
1977	Dietrich Thurau	Germany
1978	Henk Lubberding	Netherlands
1979	Jean-René Bernaudeau	France
1980	Johan van der Velde	Netherlands
1981	Peter Winnen	Netherlands
1982	Phil Anderson	Australia
1983	Laurent Fignon	France
1984	Greg LeMond	USA
1985	Fabio Parra	Colombia
1986	Andrew Hampsten	USA
1987	Raúl Alcalá	Mexico
1988	Erik Breukink	Netherlands
1989	Fabrice Philipot	France
1990	Gilles Delion	France
1991	Álvaro Mejía	Colombia
1992	Eddy Bouwmans	Netherlands
1993	Antonio Martin Velasco	Spain
1994	Marco Pantani	Italy
1995	Marco Pantani	Italy
1996	Jan Ullrich	Germany
1997	Jan Ullrich	Germany
1998	Jan Ullrich	Germany
1999	Benoît Salmon	France
2000	Francisco Mancebo	Spain
2001	Óscar Sevilla	Spain
2002	Ivan Busso	Italy
2003	Denis Menchov	Russia
2004	Vladamir Karpets	Russia
2005	Yaroslav Popovych	Ukraine
2006	Damiano Cunego	Italy
2007	Alberto Contador	Spain
2008	Andy Schleck	Netherlands
2009	Andy Schleck	Netherlands
2010	Andy Schleck	Netherlands
2011	Pierre Rolland	France
2012	Tejay van Garderen	USA

❋ YELLOW JERSEYS EIGHT YEARS APART ❋

The 1947 Tour de France was the first to be held since 1939 and at the end of Stage 2 René Vietto, the hot favourite to win in 1947 and runner-up in 1939, took over the yellow jersey. Vietto had worn yellow in previous Tours but never in Paris. Sadly for Vietto the trend continued in 1947.

❋ MASS ELIMINATION AVOIDED ❋

Belgium's Lucien Van Impe won the 1976 Tour de France and six King of the Mountains titles (1971, 1972, 1975, 1977, 1981 and 1983). After Spain's Luis Ocaña attacked on the second climb of Stage 14, the Portillon, Van Impe's team manager Cyrille Guimard told him to go after the Spaniard. When Van Impe expressed his reluctance to chase it is said that Guimard told Van Impe that if he didn't go after Ocaña, he would run him off the road with his car. Van Impe set off in pursuit of the 1973 Tour winner and caught Ocaña on the Peyresourde, the day's penultimate climb. On the final climb, the Pla d'Adet up to St Lary-Soulon, Van Impe sped away from Ocaña to win the stage and claim the yellow jersey. The Ocaña–Van Impe duel was so fierce that 45 of the remaining 94 riders in the Tour finished outside the time limit. The Raleigh team manager Peter Post spoke to the Tour organisers on behalf of the riders requesting that they waive the elimination rule for the stage. Much to the relief of the riders the rule was indeed waived.

❋ PRIZES GALORE ❋

At the 1972 Tour de France, in addition to the traditional four jerseys, awards were presented for elegance, teamwork, "combativity", ie fighting spirit, good humour, the fastest stage of the Tour, the first to the top of the highest point of the Tour, the best team and the most Hot Spot sprints, as well as for General Classification, points, mountains and the Combine award for best overall.

❋ A TOUR OF NATIONS ❋

In the 1948 Tour de France, there were four regional French teams, two Italian teams, two Belgian teams and an international team made up of Italians, a Pole, Swiss and Belgians to make up the 120-man peloton.

✳ THE BIRTH OF THE *MAILLOT JAUNE* ✳

History relates that during the rest-day between Stages 10 and 11 of the 1919 Tour de France, Henri Desgrange was asked by the journalists for some way to identify who was actually leading the race. Desgrange, always ready to maximise publicity for his race, presented the Tour leader, Eugène Christophe, with a yellow jersey. Whereas today's yellow jerseys are presented in a post-stage ceremony in front of the TV cameras, this first presentation was made without any particular ceremony. Desgrange chose yellow because it was the colour *L'Auto*, his sports paper and sponsor of the Tour, was printed on. Consequently the *maillot jaune* was born although Philippe Thys claimed that he was asked to wear a yellow jersey by Desgrange during the 1913 Tour.

✳ TOUR SPOKESMEN (42) ✳

"Yellow wakes me up in the morning. Yellow gets me on the bike every day. Yellow has taught me the true meaning of sacrifice. Yellow makes me suffer. Yellow is the reason I am here."
Lance Armstrong

✳ JAJA RETIRES ✳

In 2002, Laurent Jalabert said *au revoir* to the Tour de France prior to the final stage into Paris and over the finish line on the Champs-Elysées after a second consecutive King of the Mountains title. A delighted Jalabert, who retained the polka dot jersey he won in 2001, said: "I've never been a winged climber. I regard this climber's jersey as a symbol of my combativeness. This shirt is the one for the strategist. The bold one. Two years in a row I have proven that you don't need to be the first on the Tourmalet or Galibier to win this jersey. Anyone who can ride offensively can obtain this jersey. Like my last rival in the Alps, Mario Aerts. I leave this last Tour with a trophy. That was what I was aiming for at the start in Luxembourg; even though I didn't get that stage win. I'm looking forward to the final podium underneath the Arc de Triomphe on the Champs-Elysées. I've always hoped to finish my career with something as tangible as this jersey. Fit for a winner. Until the World Championships I will keep on racing focused. But even a rainbow jersey won't make me change my mind. It is time to share the life of my family. I truly hope I will be spoken of as 'Jaja' in thirty years from now, like Poulidor is still called 'Poupou' by the public. That is the nicest proof of having done something good on the bike."

✻ TOUR RETURNS AFTER A CENTURY AWAY ✻

The final stage of the 2003 Centenary Tour, Stage 20, took the riders from the little village of Ville d'Avray to the Champs-Elysées. The last time Ville d'Avray hosted a stage finish was exactly a century earlier when the winner of the first Tour de France, Maurice Garin, crossed the line the victor.

✻ FIRST BELGIAN TOUR WINNER ✻

In 1912 Odile Defraye became the first Belgian rider to win the Tour de France and only the second non-French winner of the race after François Faber from Luxembourg rode to victory in 1909. Although the French public did not like Defraye and objected to the collusion among the Belgian riders in the race, he received a hero's welcome when he returned to his home country. Defraye finished the 1912 Tour with 49 points while his nearest challenger, Eugène Christophe, finished with 108 points. Although the points gap between the two riders was huge it is interesting to note that had the race been awarded on time alone and not points, Christophe would have won the Tour. There is also one unique achievement by Defraye that may never be matched. He entered the Tour de France on nine occasions, and went past the halfway mark only twice. In 1914, he withdrew on Stage 10 (of 15), so the only time he completed the course he won the Tour (and he won his only stages – three of them).

✻ THREE YELLOW JERSEYS AWARDED ✻

Following the conclusion of Stage 7 of the 1929 Tour de France, Nicolas Frantz, André Leducq and Victor Fontan were all members of the winning break and exactly tied for the same time. Back then the Tour did not have any rules in place to decide upon ties, so three yellow jerseys were awarded.

✻ ENGLAND'S YOUNG HOPE ✻

The 1994 7.2-kilometre prologue in Lille marked Chris Boardman's first day in his first Tour de France. The young English rider rode exceptionally well and exceptionally fast, and won the prologue, beating three-times Tour winner Miguel Indurain by 15 seconds and Toni Rominger by 19 seconds. He claimed the yellow jersey to become the first Englishman to wear it since Tommy Simpson, 32 years earlier.

✷ THE FIRST PROFESSIONAL TOUR ✷

In 1930 Henri Desgrange discarded the team time trials and reverted to mass-starts. He also permitted riders to receive help with bicycle repairs, and dispensed with the rule whereby a rider had to finish a stage with the bike he started with. In effect Desgrange's new rule changes after 27 years of strictness meant he had accepted that professional bicycle racing is a sport contested by teams and won by individuals. The 1930 Tour de France included many giants of the sport: France's Marcel Bidot, Victor Fontan, André Leducq, Antonin Magne, Pierre Magne and Charles Pélissier; Italy's Alfredo Binda and Learco Guerra; Belgium's Louis Delannoy, Joseph Demuysère and Aimé Dossche. However, only one man could occupy the top position on the podium in Paris, and André Leducq won the first of his two overall yellow jerseys.

✷ TREBLE FOR BIG MIG ✷

In 1993 Miguel Indurain won his third consecutive overall yellow jersey in the Tour de France. His general classification time was 95 hours 57 minutes 9 seconds, and he finished 4 minutes 59 seconds ahead of the runner-up, Toni Rominger.

✷ HOLDER ABANDONS TOUR ✷

On Stage 3 of the 1924 Tour de France Henri Pélissier, winner of the Tour in 1923, was stopped a couple of times by a race commissar who proceeded to count how many jerseys the rider was wearing. On the previous day Pélissier had discarded a jersey and incurred a penalty. A furious Pélissier, along with his brother Francis and Maurice Ville, withdrew from the race as it went through the town of Coutances. Some time later when the peloton passed through the city of Granville, Albert Londres, a journalist on the Tour, noticed that the Pélissier brothers were not in the race. When he discovered they had quit he got in his car and drove to Coutances where he found the Pélissier brothers and Ville drinking hot chocolate at a bar in the railway station. Henri Pélissier gave Londres a scoop of a story when he lifted the lid on what went on in the world's most famous bike race. He talked about the doping products the riders took to help them through the long stages and showed Londres cocaine for his eyes, boxes of pills and chloroform for the gums. Londres' scoop, entitled *Les Forçats de la Route* (Prisoners of the Road), caused a huge sensation among Tour followers.

❃ TOUR ASSASSINATION ❃

On 28 June 1914, the 12th Tour de France rolled out of Paris. Little did the riders know that on that very same day, war was on Europe's doorstep. At approximately 11am, Archduke Franz Ferdinand of Austria and his wife were assassinated in Sarajevo by the Serbian secret agent Gavrilo Princip. This event triggered a tragic series of ultimatums between the great powers of Europe. On 26 July 1914, Philippe Thys became the second Belgian rider to win the Tour and eight days later Germany declared war on France and invaded Belgium.

❃ TOUR SPOKESMEN (43) ❃

"It never gets easier. You just go faster."
Greg LeMond

❃ BONUS TIMES ❃

In 1932 the Tour organisers added more and larger time bonuses for stage wins. A stage-winner was now rewarded with a huge four minutes, second place got two minutes and third place received a one-minute bonus.

❃ DEFLATED BUT VICTORIOUS ❃

When he suffered a flat tyre on the descent of the Vars while leading Stage 14 of the 1938 Tour de France, Gino Bartali (Italy) had to sit at the roadside and watch his teammate Mario Vicini ride past him. However when he got back in the saddle he soon found himself alone again on the Izoard and stayed ahead for the rest of the stage, finishing 5 minutes 18 seconds ahead of Vicini. Bartali moved into yellow and remained in yellow for the rest of the Tour.

❃ TENTH TIME LUCKY ❃

In 1980, the Dutch rider Joop Zoetemelk left the Miko team and switched to TI-Raleigh. This was the 33-year-old Zoetemelk's tenth attempt to win the Tour in which he had finished runner-up four times, starting with his maiden Tour in 1970 when he finished second to Eddy Merckx. Zoetemelk had also finished fourth twice and fifth once. However, it was to be tenth time lucky for the Dutchman as he won the 1980 Tour de France.

❊ LEADER BUYS A NEW WHEEL EN ROUTE ❊

François Faber from Luxembourg, the first non-French winner of the Tour in 1909, won the last two stages of his career in 1914, Stages 13 and 14, but he did not win the race. The man who was leading the 1914 Tour, Philippe Thys (Peugeot), was almost forced out when, chasing Faber on Stage 14, he completely ruined one of his wheels. Rather than attempting to repair it, Thys gambled on purchasing a new wheel from a local shop, thus incurring a time penalty. The alternative for the Belgian, however, was to lose a few hours attempting to fix the broken wheel. Thys was handed a 30-minute penalty that still kept him in the lead, though his advantage was a slender 1 minute, 50 seconds over Henri Pélissier. But Thys held on to his lead on the final stage to Paris and won a second consecutive Tour de France, matching the achievement of Lucien Petit-Breton, who also won back-to-back Tours, in 1907 and 1908.

❊ SOMETHING FISHY GOING ON ❊

Stage 9 of the 1965 Tour de France took the riders from Dax to Bagnères de Bigorre in the Pyrenees. It was a sweltering day with climbs over the Aubisque and the Tourmalet. Approximately three kilometres into the Aubisque Vittorio Adorni, the favourite to win the Tour, climbed off his bike and clutched his stomach in agony. He quit the race, as too did Lucien Aimar, Peter Post, Julien Stevens, Federico Bahamontes and the *maillot jaune*, Bernard Van de Kerckhove. A total of 10 riders quit that day and many suspected that a doping programme had gone wrong in circumstances similar to the Wiel's Affair during the 1962 Tour, when the team claimed to have eaten bad fish at their hotel when there was in fact no fish on the menu. Nothing was ever proven about the doping claims in either Tour.

❊ *TIFOSI* SALUTE LION KING ❊

Stage 13 of the 1992 Tour de France, 254.5 kilometres from St Gervais to Sestriere in Italy, was a torturous one even for the world's best climbers. The riders faced the Saisies (Category 2), the Cornet de Roseland (Category 1), the challenging Iseran (*Hors Catégorie*), Mont-Cenis (Category 1) and the Category 1 climb to the finish at Sestriere. An absolutely superb break by Claudio Chiappucci, with 125 kilometres to the finish, earned him the adulation of the *tifosi*, the Italian fans, when he crossed the line in Sestriere.

❋ GREAT TOURS DE FRANCE (9): 1996 ❋

Denmark had its first Tour winner in 1996, Bjarne Riis, though it was tarnished by his admission, 11 years later, that he had taken the blood doping agent EPO during the event. There were only four mountain stages on the Tour and Riis won two of them, Stage 9 to Sestrieres and Stage 16 to Hautacam. It was a very closely contested Tour throughout, though Riis didn't relinquish the yellow jersey after the run to Sestrieres. Jan Ullrich was within 101 seconds by the time the riders rode along the Champs-Elysées, but the 10th-placed finisher Toni Rominger was a little more than 10 minutes behind the German. The sprint champion Erik Zabel won the first of his record six green jerseys in 1996.

Rank	Name	Country	Time
1.	Bjarne Riis	Denmark	95h 57' 16"
2.	Jan Ullrich	Germany	+1' 41"
3.	Richard Virenque	France	+4' 37"
4.	Laurent Dufaux	Switzerland	+5' 53"
5.	Peter Luttenberger	Austria	+7' 07"
6.	Luc Leblanc	France	+10' 03"
7.	Piotr Ugrumov	Latvia	+10' 04"
8.	Fernando Escartin	Spain	+10' 26"
9.	Abraham Olano	Spain	+11' 00"
10.	Toni Rominger	Switzerland	+11' 53"

Did You Know That?
Jan Ullrich, who won the white jersey in 1996, 1997 and 1998, is one of four riders to win the overall Tour and the young rider's classification in the same year (he did it in 1997).

❋ THE 2001 TOUR IN PERSPECTIVE ❋

The 2001 Tour de France, the 88th Tour, covered a distance of 3,455.7 kilometres (average stage distance: 173.1km), over 20 stages in total. Of these 10 were flat stages, three medium mountain stages, four high mountain stages, two individual time trials and one team time trial. Stage 1 began on 7 July with an 8.2km prologue on a totally flat road winding around the port and back along to finish on the beachfront promenade of Dunkirk, le Digue de Mer. The opening prologue was won by France's Christophe Moreau (Festina) in a time of 9.20 (52.714 km/h).

❋ TOUR LEGENDS (10) – BRADLEY WIGGINS ❋

Bradley Wiggins, the son of former Australian racing cyclist Gary Wiggins, was born on 28 March 1980 in Ghent, Belgium, before growing up in Kilburn, north-west London. He followed in his father's pedal straps and represented Camden in the 1992 London Youth Games. In 1997, he won gold in the individual pursuit at the Junior World Track Championships in Cuba.

More medals followed as Bradley reached adulthood: in September 2001, it was silver in the team pursuit at the Track Cycling World Championships; silvers for England in the team and individual pursuits at the 1992 Commonwealth Games; in 2003, there was gold in the individual pursuit and silver in the team pursuit at the Track Cycling World Championships. In the Tour de l'Avenir, Wiggins claimed his first-ever stage victory in 2003, winning the opening stage – he also won Stage 8 of the event in 2005.

Equally at home on the track or the road, Bradley made his Tour de France debut in 2006 riding for the Cofidis team and returned indoors in 2007 where he won gold medals in both team and individual pursuit in the Track Cycling World Championships. In the Olympic Games, Bradley added two gold medals (in the Individual and Team Pursuit, the latter in a world record time) at Beijing 2008 to his earlier haul of Team Pursuit bronze at Sydney 2000 and gold (Individual Pursuit), silver (Team Pursuit) and bronze (Madison) at Athens 2004.

Returning to road racing, Wiggins finished fourth in the 2009 Tour de France, equalling the highest-placed finish by a British rider in Tour history. A member of the new Team Sky outfit, he could not replicate his Tour de France success in 2010, finishing 23rd overall, and a terrible crash forced him to abandon in 2011 with a broken collarbone.

In the run-up to the 2012 Tour de France, Wiggins won two stages and took overall victory in the Tour de Romandie. After finishing third on Stage 7, Wiggins donned the coveted Tour de France yellow jersey – only the fifth British rider to wear the *maillot jaune* – and never relinquished it. He thus became the first British rider to win the world's most famous cycle race. He also claimed his first two Tour stage wins.

Wiggins has twice appeared in the New Year Honours list, receiving the OBE in 2005 and CBE in 2009. His glorious 2012 campaign ended with his selection as the BBC Sports Personality of the Year and, two weeks later, he was awarded a knighthood in the New Year Honours list.

Did You Know That?
The French sports newspaper *L'Equipe* described Bradley Wiggins's trademark sideburns as "the most famous sideburns since Elvis Presley".

✷ THE COPPI AFFAIR ✷

Some writers claim that Fausto Coppi, winner of the Tour de France in 1952, did not enter the 1953 Tour because he refused to ride in the same team as his compatriot Gino Bartali. Others suggest that Coppi's main focus in 1953 was to win the World Road Championships that were to be held at the end of August in Lugano. It was further suggested that if he rode in the 1953 Tour it would interfere with his preparation for the World Road Championships. As it turned out Coppi was crowned World Champion in Lugano, coming in alone some 6 minutes 22 seconds in front of Belgium's Germain Derycke. In a gruelling race only 27 of the 70 starters made it to the finish line in Lugano. However there were others who claimed that Coppi, a married man with a family, was having an affair with a woman later dubbed by the press as "The Woman in White" and that racing in the 1953 Tour would keep him away from his newfound love. Sadly, the 1952 Tour de France was his third and final appearance in the world's most famous bike race.

✷ TOUR SPOKESMEN (44) ✷

"There are no races. Only lotteries."
Jacques Anquetil

✷ JUMPING 46 PLACES TO YELLOW ✷

Following Stage 7 of the 1956 Tour de France, Roger Walkowiak (France Nord-Est-Centre regional team) took over the leader's yellow jersey and went on to claim victory in Paris. Amazingly, Walkowiak's best-ever previous Tour performance was 47th in the 1953 Tour.

✷ CHARLY BOY ✷

Charly Gaul of Luxembourg, regarded generally by many sports writers as the best Tour climber of the 1950s, made his Tour debut in 1952. Indeed, many commentators regard Gaul as the greatest climber ever, despite the fact that he won only two King of the Mountains polka dot jerseys (1955, 1956).

❋ BARTALI SEEKS GOD'S HELP ❋

Stage 7 of the 1948 Tour de France took the peloton from Biarritz over the Aubisque to Lourdes. Gino Bartali (Italy) won the stage and being very religious, he took the opportunity to say a prayer at the Holy Shrine of Lourdes and asked the Pope for a special blessing for both himself and his team. Bartali went on to win the 1948 Tour de France, his second overall yellow jersey victory coming 10 years after his first.

❋ COUNTING THE TIME ❋

The results of the first two Tours de France in 1903 and 1904 were calculated based on time, but following the wholesale cheating scandal of 1904, Henri Desgrange changed to a points-based system in 1905. However the points-based system was unpopular with the public, and often resulted in unexciting racing. Under the points-based system a gap of one second had the same effect on the overall lead as one of four hours, so riders could allow another rider to build a substantial break without it resulting in a major difference in the overall standings. Indeed Odile Defraye won the 1912 Tour under the points-based system despite the fact that second-placed Eugène Christophe completed the Tour in less time than Defraye. Therefore in 1913 Desgrange reverted to calculating the winner of the Tour using the elapsed time method. However, many cynics at the time felt that Desgrange, who was fiercely nationalistic, was merely attempting to prevent Belgian riders from dominating his race given that Defraye was the first Belgian to win the Tour de France.

❋ MONSTER GEAR ❋

Greg LeMond (ADR) powered a monster 54 x 12 gear on his bike, driving it a steaming 54.545 kilometres an hour, to record the fastest time trial ever ridden in the history of the Tour de France (at the time) when he clinched overall victory on the Champs-Elysées in 1989. A few months later LeMond matched his second Tour win by claiming his second World Championship.

❋ TOUR SPOKESMEN (45) ❋

"I have dreamed many sporting dreams, but never have I conceived of anything as worthy as this reality."
Henri Desgrange, the "father of the Tour"

❋ COMBINE CLASSIFICATION SHELVED ❋

The 1975 Tour de France ditched the Combine classification and introduced a new jersey which was awarded to the Best Young Rider. Ironically, the Best Young Rider wore a white jersey, the colour previously worn by the Combine leader.

❋ VICTORY SCARS ❋

Going into Stage 14 of the 1921 Tour de France, the penultimate stage, Léon Scieur (La Sportive) held a lead of 21 minutes 47 seconds over his nearest challenger for the overall yellow jersey, Hector Heusghem (La Sportive). Scieur's rear wheel however snapped, with 11 broken spokes. At the time the Tour rules stipulated that a rider could replace a wheel only if no repair was possible, but he must first seek and obtain the permission of a race commissar. With no commissar in sight Scieur replaced the broken wheel and strapped it to his back. He rode for more than 300 kilometres with the wheel on his back to show the race officials at the finish line that he had good reason to fit a new wheel. For many years afterwards, the scars left on his back by the sprocket were still visible. Scieur remained in yellow and won the Tour over Heusghem at 18 minutes 36 seconds.

❋ A CHANGE OF PYRENEAN SCENERY ❋

In 1928 Tour boss Henri Desgrange changed the route of the first Pyrenean stage from the one he had used since 1913. As a result, instead of the usual Bayonne to Luchon route he chose to start at Hendaye and crossed the Aubisque and the Tourmalet before arriving at Luchon. In the process Desgrange omitted the Aspin and the Peyresourde.

❋ ANOTHER CROSS-CHANNEL TRIP ❋

In 1994 the Tour de France made another crossing of the English Channel, for the first time since 1974. Chris Boardman, who won the opening prologue but lost his yellow jersey on day 2, was anxious to claim the *maillot jaune* on home soil. However, the best he could manage was a fourth-place finish in one of the two stages held in England. Ironically when the Tour returned to France, it was a British rider, Sean Yates, who donned the *maillot jaune* on the Tour's first day back.

✻ GREAT CLIMBS (10) – MONT VENTOUX ✻

Mont Ventoux is the most iconic mountain climbed on the Tour de France. As with all *hors catégorie* challenges, it does not appear in every Tour, but the man who wears the yellow jersey in Paris after going over the top of "the Giant of Provence" automatically gains the respect of the Tour cognoscenti. Ventoux's name dates back to Gallic times, possibly from *Ven-Top* (snowy peak) or Vintur (Gaul god of summits). A chapel, dedicated to the Holy Cross was built at the summit, probably in the 15th century, and a 50m-tall communications mast went up in the 1960s.

Location: The département of Vaucluse and region of Provence in SE France.

Nearest town: Bédoin.

Height: The peak is 2,067m, but the stage finish is at 1,909m.

Gradient: The average gradient of the ascent of Ventoux from Bédoin is 7.43 percent, a climb of 1,617m over 21.825km.

Characteristics: There is no little or no vegetation on the upper reaches of Mont Ventoux, giving it an almost lunar feel. The highest wind recorded on Ventoux is 320 kmh (200 mph); on more than 240 days per year it tops 90 kmh (56 mph).

Tour visits: 14 in total, eight as a stage finish, six in mid-stage.

Multiple winners: None (either as a stage-winner or leading over the summit).

Conquerors of the peak: Lucien Lazarides (1951), Jean Robic (1952), Louison Bobet (1955), Charly Gaul (1958*), Raymond Poulidor (1965*), Julio Jímenez (1967), Eddy Merckx (1970*), Bernard Thévenet (1972*), Gonzalo Aja (1974), Jean-François Bernard (1987*), Eros Poli (1994), Marco Pantani (2000*), Richard Virenque (2002*), Juan Manuel Gárate (2009*).
* = *stage finished at the summit*

Did You Know That?
Tragically, on 13 July 1967, British rider Tommy Simpson died climbing Mont Ventoux. There is now a memorial to Simpson, close to where he fell.

✳ FRENCH ADOPT THE 'COPPI PLAN' ✳

Three French national team riders occupied the top three places in Stage 13 of the 1953 Tour de France: Nello Lauredi (first), Raphaël Géminiani (second) and Louison Bobet (third). That evening as the team was having dinner in their hotel, Bobet accused Lauredi and Géminiani of collaborating to prevent him from winning the stage. Géminiani knocked the dinner table over and grabbed his fork at which point Bobet ran away in tears. Marcel Bidot, the team manager, called an urgent team meeting and simply asked his riders who among them could win the Tour and claim the yellow jersey for the team in Paris. Only one man raised his hand, Bobet, who openly stated that he could win the Tour if his teammates rallied around him and protected him. The French riders adopted the "Coppi Plan" as Bobet promised the other riders on the team all of his Tour prize money if he won. A formal contract was drawn up and Bobet rode to victory to claim the first of three consecutive Tour wins.

✳ THE PELOTON OF CHAMPIONS ✳

All Tour winners from 1905 (Louis Trousselier) to 1923 (Henri Pélissier) started the 1914 Tour de France except René Pottier (winner in 1906), who was dead. Philippe Thys won the 1914 Tour de France, his second in succession, while Lucien Buysse, who would win the Tour in 1926, also started the 1914 Tour. In total 11 of the 1914 starting peloton were past or future Tour de France winners.

✳ TOUR'S FIRST CONSECUTIVE HAT-TRICK ✳

In 1955 Louison Bobet (France) became the first rider in the history of the Tour de France to win the race three years in a row. During his career Bobet won many of the world's other famous cycle races, including Milan–San Remo, Tour of Lombardy, Tour of Flanders, the World Championships, Grand Prix de Nations, the Tour of Luxembourg and Paris–Roubaix. Bobet must without doubt be regarded as one of the greatest riders of all time.

✳ A DOPEY RIDER ✳

Hennes "Hans" Junkermann was handed a 10-minute penalty after Stage 7 of the 1972 Tour de France after testing positive for dope. The German rider, one of the protagonists in the 1962 Tour's "Wiel's Affair", abandoned the race after Stage 13.

❋ BARTALI'S TOUR BIRTHDAY PRESENT ❋

Stage 16 of the 1949 Tour de France, from Cannes to Briançon, was the first day in the Alps with the Allos, Vars and Izoard climbs ahead of the riders. On the Izoard Fausto Coppi (Italy) and the 1948 Tour de France winner, Gino Bartali (Italy), broke away and established a sizeable lead over the chasing peloton which included the 1947 Tour winner, Jean Robic (France), and they advanced even further ahead of the rest of the field. When Bartali flatted on the Izoard, his teammate waited for him. When the dynamic pair resumed racing they destroyed the chasing Robic who came in 5 minutes behind them, while the rest of the peloton didn't cross the finish line for another 90 seconds. As it was Bartali's 35th birthday Coppi, feeling supremely confident of his own ability, allowed his teammate to take the stage victory. Following the stage Bartali remained ahead of Coppi in the GC and donned the yellow jersey. That left Coppi sitting pretty in second place at 1 minute, 22 seconds behind his Tuscan teammate.

❋ THE WAR-TORN TOUR DE FRANCE ❋

The 1919 Tour de France started just seven months after the First World War came to an end on 11 November 1918 ("the eleventh hour of the eleventh day of the eleventh month"). With the riders unable to adequately prepare for the 15 stages over 5,560 kilometres across the war-torn roads of France, the net result was the slowest Tour ever, 24.056 kph. Of the 67 riders who entered, only 10 made it to Paris.

❋ DIY ON THE ROAD ❋

In 1929 Henri Desgrange decided to revert to an old rule of his requiring riders to fix their own flat tyres.

❋ THE STOP-LOSS RULE ❋

A "stop-loss" rule was introduced to the 2004 Tour de France for the team time trial. Under the rule the most time a rider could lose in the team chrono event was 3 minutes. The founder of the Tour de France, Henri Desgrange, would have fully approved of this rule given that he hated to see a weak rider get too much help from a strong team or conversely, a strong rider held back by a weak team.

✻ TOUR SPOKESMEN (46) ✻

"I am, like everyone in the country, absolutely delighted. Bradley Wiggins has scaled one of the great heights of British sporting achievement. To be the first British person in 109 years to win the Tour de France is an immense feat of physical and mental ability and aptitude. I think the whole country wants to say 'well done, brilliant'."

British Prime Minister David Cameron, asked for his opinion of Bradley Wiggins's victory in the 2012 Tour de France

✻ THE FIRST ENGLISHMAN TO WEAR YELLOW ✻

Tom Simpson, the first British rider to wear the yellow jersey in the Tour de France, died on the ascent of Mount Ventoux during Stage 13 of the 1967 Tour, a 211.5-kilometre ride from Marseille to Carpentras. Even before the start of the fateful stage, Tour doctor Pierre Dumas felt that the weather could cause the death of any rider taking performance-enhancing drugs, and tragically Simpson had been using amphetamines. Simpson rode in seven Tours de France:

1960:	29th overall
1961:	Did Not Finish (DNF)
1962:	6th overall and one day in yellow
1964:	14th overall
1965:	(DNF)
1966:	(DNF)
1967:	(DNF)

Did You Know That?
Simpson's career record included victories in the Tour of Flanders, Paris–Nice, Bordeaux–Paris, Milan–San Remo, Tour of Lombardy and the Brussels six-day with Peter Post as his partner. In addition, in 1965, Simpson became the first British rider to win the Road Race World Championship.

✻ RIDERS RELEGATED ✻

When the peloton came in 30 minutes behind the first three on Stage 12 of the 1921 Tour, Henri Desgrange was so furious with Firmin Lambot and Louis Mottiat for not chasing down Honoré Barthélémy, Hector Heusghem and Léon Scieur that he relegated them to last place in the stage for their failure to ride competitively.

❊ BARTALI BEATEN UP ❊

Stage 11 of the 1950 Tour de France took the riders into the Pyrenees from Pau to St Gaudens, a 230-kilometre trek crossing the Aubisque, the Tourmalet and the Aspin. Along the route stood unhappy French fans who had had to endure two successive years of Italian dominance on their Tour following Gino Bartali's win in 1948 and Fausto Coppi's success in 1949 (Coppi was injured in 1950 and did not compete in the Tour). As the riders crested the Tourmalet, a number of people at the side of the road began to throw stones, bottle caps and whatever they could lay their hands on at the riders. As the lead group of riders comprising Bartali, Louison Bobet, Stan Ockers and Jean Robic reached the summit of the Aspin, they found their way blocked by a photographer who was standing on their side of the road. Bartali and Robic crashed trying to avoid the photographer and Robic ruined his front wheel. Some fans helped the two fallen riders get back in their saddles and as Bartali attempted to remount his bike he was kicked and punched. Jacques Goddet, the Tour boss, arrived at the scene and started to beat the drunken spectators back with a large stick. Bartali got his revenge on the unruly fans by claiming the stage victory.

❊ ANQUETIL'S CRYSTAL BALL ❊

Prior to the 1961 Tour de France Jacques Anquetil (France) boldly predicted that he would take the yellow jersey on the opening day and wear it all the way to Paris. André Darrigade (France) won the opening stage but then that same afternoon Anquetil quite easily won the 28.5-kilometre time trial at Versailles, and saw the first part of his bold prediction come true by taking the *maillot jaune* from Darrigade on the first day of the Tour. Anquetil went on to fulfil his prediction of acquiring the yellow jersey on the opening day and wearing it all the way to Paris.

❊ RACE GROUPS ❊

In 1921 the Tour de France was divided into Group 1 and Group 2 riders, with Group 1 containing the superior, sponsored riders. However Henri Desgrange was so angry with the Group 1 riders for not racing hard on Stage 12 that he permitted the Group 2 riders to start Stage 13 before their counterparts. The stage was won by Félix Sellier, a Group 2 rider, while the first Group 1 rider finished 30 minutes behind him.

❋ GREEN JERSEY GOES DOWN UNDER ❋

The final stage of the 2003 Centenary Tour de France ended in a massive bunch sprint on the Champs-Elysées and was won by Jean-Patrick Nazon (Jean Delatour). The French rider took full advantage of the battle for the green jersey between Robbie McEwen (Lotto Domo) and Baden Cooke (FDJeux.com) for the green jersey, and shot up the centre of the road as the two Australians eyed each other up. Cooke crossed the line in second place, which was enough to give him the *maillot vert* by just two points over McEwen.

❋ TWO BIKES, ONE RIDER ❋

Going into Stage 10 of the 1929 Tour de France, from Luchon to Perpignan, the yellow jersey leader Victor Fontan crashed badly after either hitting a dog or falling into a gutter by the side of the road (reports on this differ). Although unhurt following his crash, his forks were broken and so he had no choice but to knock on doors in the nearest village in search of a replacement bike. He eventually found one but as per the Tour's rules he had to finish the stage with the equipment he started with, and so off he set in pursuit of the leaders on the borrowed bike with his own bike strapped to his back. Fontan rode bravely for 145 kilometres in the high Pyrenees but with the added weight of his own bike it was all too much for the 37-year-old and he was forced to abandon the Tour and sat at the side of the road in tears. Desgrange felt for Fontan and the following year he changed the rules to permit riders to get new bikes from the following team vehicles.

❋ TOUR SPOKESMEN (47) ❋

"We're going to start drawing the raffle numbers now."
Bradley Wiggins standing on top of the presentation podium after being presented with the most coveted trophy in professional cycling for winning the 2012 Tour de France

❋ JESUS WINS ❋

On Stage 10 of the 1953 Tour de France, which took the race from Pau over the Aubisque and then over the Second Category climb to the finish at Cauterets, Spain's Jesus Lorono was first over the Aubisque and soloed in for the stage victory.

❋ SUPER ANDY ❋

Andy Hampsten won his first stage in the Tour de France when he claimed the most prestigious of all the mountain stages, the classic Alpine crossing over the Galibier, the Croix de Fer and a finish on l'Alpe d'Huez in the 1992 race. All three mountains on Stage 14 were *hors catégorie* climbs. Hampsten's victory shot him up to third place overall in the GC and the hopes of a podium finish in Paris. However, when the Tour arrived in Paris Hampsten finished fourth overall, three minutes behind third-placed Gianni Bugno.

❋ MOST *HORS CATÉGORIE* CLIMBS ❋

Mountain	No. of HC climbs	Total climbs	Ht (m)	First HC	Most recent
Alpe d'Huez	23	27	1,860	1979	2011
Col du Tourmalet	20	54	2,115	1980	2012
Col du Galibier	18	32	2,645	1979	2011
Col de la Madelaine	15	23	1,993	1980	2012
Col d'Aubisque	12	47	1,709	1980	2012
Col de la Croix-de-Fer	8	16	2,067	1989	2012
Luz Ardiden	7	7	1,715	1985	2011
Col d'Izoard	6	23	2,360	1986	2011
Col de Joux-Plane	6	11	1,691	1981	2006
Plateau de Beille	5	5	1,780	1998	2011
Mont Ventoux	4	14	1,909	1987	2009
Pla d'Adet	4	9	1,669	1981	2005
La Plagne	4	4	1,980	1984	2002
Hautacam	4	4	1,560	1994	2008

NOTE: *The organisers of the Tour de France established the* hors catégorie *level of difficulty in 1979.*

❋ SWISS TOUR DE FORCE ❋

The 1954 Swiss team that entered the Tour de France was a formidable team that included two Tour winners, Ferdy Kübler (1950) and Hugo Koblet (1951), as well as that year's Giro d'Italia winner Carlo Clerici. They also had the very accomplished Fritz Schaer who had worn the *maillot jaune* for a while in the 1953 Tour de France and claimed the sprinter's *maillot vert* the same year. Louison Bobet (France) won the 1954 Tour while Kübler was second and Schaer was third. Kübler won the green jersey.

❋ SCOTLAND THE BRAVE ❋

Stage 10 of the 1983 Tour de France took the riders into the mountains for the first day and the only Pyrenean stage that year, a 201-kilometre trek from Pau to Bagnères de Luchon. During the stage the riders had to climb the Aubisque, the Tourmalet, the Aspin and the Peyresourde. The first two climbs were rated as *hors catégorie* and the second two were difficult First Category climbs. Robert Millar won the stage in front of Pedro Delgado to become the first Scotsman to win a stage in the race's 80-year history.

❋ THE EMPEROR'S WRONG TURN ❋

At the end of Stage 2 of the 1962 Tour de France the reigning World Professional Road Race Champion, Rik Van Looy, took a wrong turn in the city of his birth, Herentals in Belgium, and missed the opportunity to win in front of his family and friends. Thankfully for Van Looy his Flandria squad made up for his embarrassment by winning that afternoon's team time trial, also held in Herentals. Van Looy was nicknamed the "Emperor of Herentals" after his home town and the authoritative way he treated his peers. He was twice World Professional Road Race Champion (1960 and 1961) and was the first cyclist to win all five of the "Monument" Classic Cycle Races, a feat since achieved by just two other riders, who are also Belgian (Roger De Vlaeminck and Eddy Merckx).

❋ TOUR SPOKESMEN (48) ❋

"Our aim is to win the Tour de France within five years."
Dave Brailsford at a press conference announcing the creation of Team Sky on 26 February 2009

❋ BOBET CLAIMS 50TH ANNIVERSARY TOUR ❋

Louison Bobet (France) won the 1953 Tour de France, the 50th Anniversary Tour. To celebrate the anniversary, a gathering of previous Tour winners was waiting to greet Bobet in the Parc de Princes velodrome for his victory lap in Paris. The inaugural Tour winner of 1903, Maurice Garin, was there, as were Gustave Garrigou, Lucien Buysse, Philippe Thys, Romain and Sylvère Maes, André Leducq, Antonin Magne, Georges Speicher, Roger Lapébie and Ferdy Kübler.

✵ TOUR JARGON BUSTER ✵

Abandon .... What a rider does when he pulls out of the Tour in progress, either for injury, illness or exhaustion.

ASO .... Amaury Sport Organisation, the group which runs the Tour.

Bonked .... Exhaustion suffered by a rider whose energy reserves are depleted.

Bonus .... Special time bonuses are given for winning sprints, either intermediate or at the finish of a stage.

Combine Competition .... This is for the best all-round rider, combining positions on the general and points classifications.

Falling off .... Similar to shelled, a rider who falls away from the rear of the peloton.

GC .... The race for the yellow jersey is decided by this, adding up the times from each stage, plus bonuses.

General Classification .... The official term for GC.

Grand Tours .... Road cycling's three biggest multi-stage events: the Tours of Italy (Giro d'Italia), France (Le Tour) and Spain (Vuelta a España), held in May, July and September, respectively.

Natural Break .... What the cameras don't film ... when a rider takes a brief comfort break.

Points .... These are awarded to the best sprinters for their finishes at the end of intermediate or stage-end sprints.

Red Number .... Awarded to the rider who spent the longest time in a breakaway on the previous stage.

Road Rash .... Cuts and grazes received by riders when they fall off their bikes at speed.

Shelled .... What happens to a rider when he can't keep up with the pack.

Time Limit .... All riders must finish a stage within a certain time, relative to the stage-winner, or be excluded from the Tour. In exceptional circumstances – such as a bad crash or conditions, the time limit may be extended or cancelled.

UCI	Union Cycliste Internationale, world cycling's governing body, overseeing and sanctioning all events, road or track.
Wheelsucker	A derogatory term for a rider who doesn't do his share of the hard work – take the lead – in a group of cyclists, especially on a breakaway.

✳ BELGIUM'S LAST ✳

Belgium's Lucien Van Impe won the 1976 Tour de France. No Belgian rider has won the overall yellow jersey since.

✳ THE *MAILLOT A POIS* ✳

The *maillot à pois* (the polka dot jersey) is awarded to the best climber in the Tour de France, better known as "The King of the Mountains". After each climb points are awarded to those riders who are first over the top. The climbs are divided into categories from 1 (most difficult) to 4 (least difficult) based on their difficulty, gradient and length. A fifth category, called *hors catégorie* (or "outside category") is an even more difficult climb than a Category 1.

✳ MASTER OF THE CHAMPS-ELYSEES ✳

Every year since 1975, the Tour de France has finished on the world-famous Avenue des Champs-Elysées. In 2009, Mark Cavendish became the first-ever British cyclist to cross the finishing line of the Tour de France when a stage finished on the Champs-Elysées. The following year he repeated the feat and in 2011, he completed a unique treble of Champs-Elysées victories. Victory on the Champs-Elysées, the mecca for all sprinters, is achieved only after a man is able to withstand crossing the chain of mountains which Le Tour puts before him and on occasion will decide the outcome of the prestigious green jersey which is awarded to the race's best sprinter. Many riders set off on the final stage of a Tour de France dreaming of crossing the finishing line before the rest of the peloton on the Champs-Elysées but only one man has ever won four stages at the most iconic of all stage finishes and that man is Mark Cavendish.

✳ SWITZERLAND FEELING YELLOW ✳

Paul Egli won Stage 1 of the 1936 Tour de France, making him the first Swiss rider in Tour history to wear the *maillot jaune*.

✻ LE GENTLEMAN ✻

After the 2011 Tour de France winner, Australia's Cadel Evans (BMC Racing Team), fell victim to several punctures on Stage 14, it was the race leader, Bradley Wiggins (Team Sky), who helped slow the pace of the peloton in order to allow Evans to catch up. Some so-called fans had thrown carpet tacks on to the road. Wiggens received praise from all quarters for his sportsmanship whilst the French public gave Wiggins the soubriquet of "Le Gentleman" for his sporting behaviour during the 2012 Tour de France.

✻ HINAULT MISSES OUT ON TREBLE ✻

In 1980 the 25-year-old Bernard Hinault was attempting to win his third consecutive Tour de France, thereby equalling the feat of Louison Bobet in becoming the youngest rider to win three Tours on the trot. That spring he had already won the Giro d'Italia and consequently he was also hoping to achieve the rare Giro–Tour double and join Fausto Coppi, Jacques Anquetil and Eddy Merckx in the history books. Alas Joop Zoetemelk spoiled his dream.

✻ THE FAMOUS FIVE ✻

Only five British riders have worn the race leader's yellow jersey in the Tour de France:

1962	Tom Simpson	1 day
1994*	Chris Boardman	3 days
1994	Sean Yates	1 day
1997	Chris Boardman	1 day
1998	Chris Boardman	2 days
2000*	David Millar	3 days
2012	Bradley Wiggins	13 days

Tour de France debut

✻ TOUR SPOKESMEN (49) ✻

"Bradley Wiggins has done something unbelievable by winning the Tour de France, but I know he will be the first to recognise that he would not have been able to achieve his victory without a terrific team behind him."
Geraint Thomas of Team Sky speaking after the end of the 2012 Tour de France

❋ KAMIKAZE KAZAK ❋

Kazakhstan's Alexandre Vinokourov won the final stage of the 2005 Tour de France, the 92nd edition of "Le Grand Boucle". "That was victory made of courage and guts – I really gave it all in the last kilometres, although I didn't think it was possible until I crossed the line," said an ecstatic Vinokourov. With 1,500 metres to go the affectionately nicknamed Kamikaze Kazakhstani buried himself in his machine and set off in pursuit of the lone breakaway rider, Bradley McGee (La Française des Jeux). Vino managed to claw back the Australian and passed both him and Fabian Cancellara for a victory on the famous Champs-Elysées.

❋ SUPERMAN WEARS YELLOW ❋

Eddy Merckx's 1974 Tour de France victory was his fifth, equalling Jacques Anquetil's record five Tour victories, but unlike the legendary Frenchman, Merckx had won every Tour de France he had entered. Merckx's eight stage victories in 1974 took him to 32, passing the record of 25 held by André Leducq. He was also the first, and to date only, man to have won the Italian, Swiss and French Tours in the same year. Merckx's achievement is superhuman because it entailed racing from 16 May to 21 July with little rest in between, and five days before the start of the 1974 Tour de France he had undergone surgery.

❋ THE TOUR'S DEVIL ❋

Dieter "Didi" Senft was born on 7 February 1952 in Reichenwald, Germany. Starting in 1993 he started to appear at the Tour de France and was always dressed in a red devil outfit and was quickly nicknamed "El Diablo" by the Tour media. He painted trident symbols on the road a few miles before the television camera following the peleton picked his distinctive frame out in the crowd at the side of the road. Fans on Le Tour love him and the many bicycles he specifically builds to bring along to each Tour de France including the largest bicycle in the world. Senft attributes the inspiration for his red devil costume to the German cycling announcer, Herbert Watterot, who called the last lap of local criterium races, "The Red Devil's Lap".

❋ TOUR'S ACE STAGE-WINNER IS ALSO-RAN ❋

Despite winning 23 stages, fourth-best in Tour de France history, Mark Cavendish's best finish is 130th in the general classificiation.

❋ GREAT TOURS DE FRANCE (10): 2011 ❋

On Bastille Day 2011, Thomas Voeckler was in the yellow jersey and France started dreaming of a first home victory in Le Tour since Bernard Hinault in 1985. A week later, Andy Schleck stormed over the Col du Galibier to win Stage 18. The next day, after France's Pierre Rolland won at l'Alpe d'Huez, Schleck took over the yellow jersey, but the next day was a time trial. Andy's lead over older brother Frank was 53 seconds, over Cadel Evans 57 seconds, and the Australian was easily the best of three against the clock. The brothers matched each other to within three seconds, but Evans was two and a half minutes faster. As Mark Cavendish sprinted over the line at the Champs-Elysées, winning the green jersey, Australia was celebrating the country's first Tour de France winner.

Rank	Name	Country	Time
1.	Cadel Evans	Australia	86h 12' 22"
2.	Andy Schleck	Luxembourg	+1' 34"
3.	Frank Schleck	Luxembourg	+2' 30"
4.	Thomas Voeckler	France	+3' 20"
5.	Samuel Sánchez	Spain	+4' 55"
6.	Damiano Cunego	Italy	+6' 05"
7.	Ivan Basso	Italy	+7' 23"
8.	Tom Danielson	USA	+8' 15"
9.	Jean-Christophe Péraud	France	+10' 11"
10.	Pierre Rolland	France	+10' 43"

Did You Know That?
At 34 years, five months and 10 days, Cadel Evans became the third-oldest man ever to win the Tour de France and the oldest since Henri Pélissier in 1923.

❋ TOUR SPOKESMEN (50) ❋

"I'm still buzzing from the Champs-Elysées, it's so quick around there. It will take a while … I'm just trying to soak up every minute of today as it goes along. It's very surreal at the moment. This sort of thing happens to other people, you never imagine it happens to you. It's incredible. I bet I'll look back in years to come and think, 'God, that was special.'"
Bradley Wiggins interviewed shortly after winning the 2012 Tour de France

☀ UCI ROAD RACE WORLD CHAMPIONS ☀

The winner of the UCI Road Race World Championship is entitled to wear the rainbow jersey in the following year's Tour de France.

Year	Winner (Nationality)	Year	Winner (Nationality)
1927	Alfredo Binda (ITA)	1974	Eddy Merckx (BEL)
1928	Georges Ronsse (BEL)	1975	Hennie Kuiper (NED)
1929	Georges Ronsse (BEL)	1976	Freddy Maertens (BEL)
1930	Alfredo Binda (ITA)	1977	Francesco Moser (ITA)
1931	Learco Guerra (ITA)	1978	Gerrie Knetemann (NED)
1932	Alfredo Binda (ITA)	1979	Jan Raas (NED)
1933	Georges Speicher (FRA)	1980	Bernard Hinault (FRA)
1934	Karel Kaers (BEL)	1981	Freddy Maertens (BEL)
1935	Jean Aerts (BEL)	1982	Giuseppe Saronni (ITA)
1936	Antonin Magne (FRA)	1983	Greg LeMond (USA)
1937	Eloi Meulenberg (BEL)	1984	Claude Criquielion (BEL)
1938	Marcel Kint (BEL)	1985	Joop Zoetemelk (NED)
1946	Hans Knecht (SUI)	1986	Moreno Argentin (ITA)
1947	Theo Middelkamp (NED)	1987	Stephen Roche (IRE)
1948	Briek Schotte (BEL)	1988	Maurizio Fondriest (ITA)
1949	Rik Van Steenbergen (BEL)	1989	Greg LeMond (USA)
1950	Briek Schotte (BEL)	1990	Rudy Dhaenens (BEL)
1951	Ferdi Kübler (SUI)	1991	Gianni Bugno (ITA)
1952	Heinz Müller (GER)	1992	Gianni Bugno (ITA)
1953	Fausto Coppi (ITA)	1993	Lance Armstrong (USA)
1954	Louison Bobet (FRA)	1994	Luc Leblanc (FRA)
1955	Stan Ockers (BEL)	1995	Abraham Olano (ESP)
1956	Rik Van Steenbergen (BEL)	1996	Johan Museeuw (BEL)
1957	Rik Van Steenbergen (BEL)	1997	Laurent Brochard (FRA)
1958	Ercole Baldini (ITA)	1998	Oscar Camenzind (SUI)
1959	André Darrigade (FRA)	1999	Oscar Friere (ESA)
1960	Rik van Looy (BEL)	2000	Romans Vainsteins (LAT)
1961	Rik van Looy (BEL)	2001	Oscar Friere (ESA)
1962	Jean Stablinski (FRA)	2002	Mario Cipollini (ITA)
1963	Benoni Beheyt (BEL)	2003	Igor Astarloa (ESP)
1964	Jan Janssen (NED)	2004	Oscar Friere (ESA)
1965	Tom Simpson (GBR)	2005	Tom Boonen (BEL)
1966	Rudi Altig (FRA)	2006	Paolo Bettini (ITA)
1967	Eddy Merckx (BEL)	2007	Paolo Bettini (ITA)
1968	Vittorio Adorni (ITA)	2008	Alessandro Ballan (ITA)
1969	Harm Ottenbros (NED)	2009	Cadel Evans (AUS)
1970	Jean-Pierre Monseré (BEL)	2010	Thor Hushovd (NOR)
1971	Eddy Merckx (BEL)	2011	Mark Cavendish (GBR)
1972	Marino Basso (ITA)	2012	Philippe Gilbert (BEL)
1973	Felice Gimondi (ITA)		

✽ DOPING TESTS INTRODUCED ✽

Tests for doping were first carried out on riders in the Tour de France following Stage 8 of the 1965 race. Incensed by the police raid on their hotels requesting them to provide urine samples, the riders, led by Jacques Anquetil, staged a strike by riding their bikes for 5 kilometres on Stage 9 before dismounting. As the riders pushed their bikes along the road they argued with the Tour organisers before finally agreeing to get back in their saddles and continue racing.

✽ BREAKING NEW GROUND IN 2013 ✽

The 100th edition of the Tour de France in 2013 saw the peloton visit Corsica for the first time. Corsica had been the only metropolitan département not previously visited by the Tour. The Tour also will remain inside French borders throughout the three weeks.

✽ ANNUS MIRABILIS FOR SIR BRADLEY ✽

For Bradley Wiggins, 2012 was a blessed year. He became the first Briton to win the Tour de France, won Olympic Games gold in the men's Time Trial at London 2012, was named BBC Sports Personality of the Year and received a knighthood in the Queen's New Year Honours list.

✽ ARMSTRONG REVEALS HIS DOPING PAST ✽

Lance Armstrong, who had been stripped of his seven Tour de France wins, plus his 22 stage wins, and been banned for life by the UCI, finally revealed his drug-taking past to the world. The Texan bared his soul to American talk show host Oprah Winfrey in a two-part interview which aired in mid-January 2013. He admitted that all the allegations made against him over the previous few years were indeed true and he had been doping systematically since returning to the saddle after winning his battle with cancer in the late 1990s.

✽ ROAD RACE/TOUR DOUBLES ✽

Only three men have won the Tour de France while wearing the rainbow jersey of the UCI Road Race world champion. Belgian Eddy Merckx, unsurprisingly, was the first man to achieve the feat, and he was followed by another five-time Tour winner Bernard Hinault of France and American Greg LeMond, who won three Tours.

✻ SELECT BIBLIOGRAPHY ✻

BOOKS

Crooked Path to Victory, The by Les Woodland, Cycle Publishing (July 2003)

Maillot Jaune by Jean-Paul Ollivier, VeloPress (June 2001)

Story of the Tour de France, The by Bill & Carol McGann, Dogear Press, Indianapolis, Indiana, USA (July 2006)

Tour de France Records by Chris Sidwells, Carlton Books (May 2012)

Tour de France: The World's Greatest Cycle Race by Margarite Lazell, Carlton Books (May 2012)

Uphill Battle: Cycling's Great Climbers by Owen Mulholland, VeloPress (May 2003)

The Unknown Tour de France by Les Woodland, Van Der Plas Publications (August 2000)

MAGAZINES

Cycle Sport
Cycling News

WEBSITES

bikeraceinfo.com
cyclinghalloffame.com
cyclingnews.com
dailypeloton.com
espn.go.com
gazzetta.it
letour.fr
memoire-du-cyclisme.net
ntlworld.com
radsport-news.com
studenttravel.about.com
torelli.com
wikipedia.org

✳ INDEX ✳